汉英对照

王芳带你读经典

READ THE CLASSICS WITH WANG FANG

伊索寓言

AESOP'S FABLES

王芳 / 主编
[古希腊] 伊索 / 著　赫涛 / 译

中信出版集团 | 北京

图书在版编目（CIP）数据

伊索寓言 : 汉英对照 / 王芳主编 ; (古希腊) 伊索著 ; 赫涛译 . -- 北京 : 中信出版社, 2021.5（2023.3 重印）
（王芳带你读经典）
ISBN 978-7-5217-2931-3

Ⅰ. ①伊… Ⅱ. ①王… ②伊… ③赫… Ⅲ. ①英语－汉语－对照读物②寓言－作品集－古希腊 Ⅳ. ①H319.4 : I

中国版本图书馆CIP数据核字(2021)第043528号

伊索寓言（汉英对照）
（王芳带你读经典）

主　　编：王芳
著　　者：[古希腊] 伊索
译　　者：赫涛
绘　　者：陈香渝　王天佑
出版发行：中信出版集团股份有限公司
（北京市朝阳区东三环北路27号嘉铭中心　邮编　100020）
承 印 者：北京盛通印刷股份有限公司

开　　本：720mm×970mm　1/16　　印　　张：13.5　　字　　数：175千字
版　　次：2021年5月第1版　　印　　次：2023年3月第7次印刷
书　　号：ISBN 978-7-5217-2931-3
定　　价：68.00元

出　　品：中信儿童书店
图书策划：如果
策划编辑：邵安　高霜月
责任编辑：谢媛媛
营销编辑：张远　邝青青
装帧设计：刘潇然
内文排版：杭州乐读文化创意有限公司

服务热线：400-600-8099
投稿邮箱：author@citicpub.com

序言

Preface

亲爱的小读者们：

很高兴能把这样一本装帧精美、内容实用的《伊索寓言》推荐给你们！

伊索是古希腊一位非常伟大的哲学家、文学家，他生活的时代和中国的孔子大概相当。公元前800年至公元前200年，被哲学家称为人类文明的“轴心时代”，是塑造人类精神和世界观的大转折时代。以苏格拉底、释迦牟尼、孔子等为代表的先哲们都生活在这个时代，他们创立了各自的思想体系。

在这些先哲中，伊索无疑是很有特点的一位，但关于他的记录少之又少。而对比同时期的孔子，我们可以较为清楚地知道孔子的出生日期，甚至还能知道孔子一生中的每一年都在做什么。但提及伊索，所有的相关记载都用了这样的词汇："约""相传""据说"……大多并不准确。

在有限的资料里，我们可以知道伊索曾经做过奴隶，受人奴役很多年。由于他博学多才，很会给别人讲故事，才最终获得了自由，而后开始周游世界，为人们讲述他从各地搜罗来的寓言故事。

尽管关于伊索的人生很多都是后人猜测的，但毋庸置疑，伊索在当时就拥有了很大的名声。他是古希腊人民心中智慧的象征，以至于后来很多人把民间收集来的小故事都称作"伊索寓言"。也就是说，我们现在看到的《伊索寓言》，很大一部分和伊索本人没有关系。

在《伊索寓言》中，每一篇小故事都蕴含着深刻的道理。阅读之后，或让你开心一笑，或让你沉静深思。

我读过很多版本的《伊索寓

言》，有相当一部分的语言是晦涩难懂的，可能它们追求的是对原文的高度还原。我认为对于你们来说，最好的读本要翻译精准，同时又具备很强的可读性，可惜这样的《伊索寓言》总是可遇而不可求。直到我遇到了中信出版集团的编辑，我们一拍即合，决心做出一本既漂亮，又读起来有趣，还拥有丰富功能性的《伊索寓言》，于是这本书就应运而生了！

在海量阅读、广泛对比了不同的版本之后，我们选择了周作人先生的翻译版本作为参考。周作人先生是文学家，也是中国现代的翻译大家，他的文风平和冲淡，清新晓畅。我们在这个版本的基础上选取了《伊索寓言》中最具代表性的篇目，尽量呈现原著的整体风貌，同时细致打磨了选篇的内容，让经典更加通俗易懂，符合家庭亲子阅读和孩子自主阅读的需求。

不仅如此，这本《伊索寓言》还是双语阅读，每一篇寓言故事都为大家提供了汉英对照。考虑到小读者们的阅读需求，英文部分还细致地整理了一份重难点词汇表，希望小读者们在阅读中不仅可以读故事，还可以学英语。

英国有一位天才小说家叫毛姆，他有一本谈及读书的随笔集叫《阅读是一座随身携带的避难所》。关于阅读，毛姆说：“人应当为了快乐而读书。”对我来说更是如此。阅读给我带来的最大收获就是教会我不要害怕寂寞。因为独处的时光更珍贵、更美，我可以安安静静地享受阅读，远离寂寞。我了解到，很多我的同龄人独自在家时，会觉得很孤单，选择无所事事地虚度时间。但我因为拥有阅读这项爱好，所以能够毫不费力地享受只有自己一个人的时光。

亲爱的小读者们，我衷心地希望大家能够从小养成爱阅读的好习惯，在阅读中捕捞智慧和灵感，获取对生活的信念和希望，长大以后，你们也会成为永远都不害怕寂寞的人。

王芳

2021 年 5 月

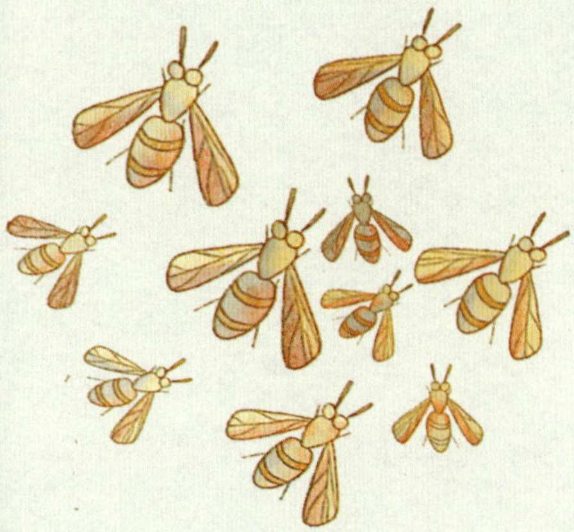

目录

Contents

阅读指南

1. 夜莺与鹰

在高高的大树上，一只**夜莺**像往常一样唱着歌。一只饥饿的**鹰**猛扑过去，一把将她抓住。临死之际，夜莺恳求鹰放过她，说自己个子太小，填不饱鹰的肚子。要是鹰觉得饿，应该找比她大的鸟来吃。鹰却回答：“如果我放弃了早已到手的食物，而去追求还看不到的东西，那我不成傻瓜了吗？”

愚蠢的人才会为了贪图看不到的利益，而放弃已经到手的东西。

双色标注
主角出场

知识岛：希腊神话里的夜莺

◎ 在希腊神话中，底比斯王后埃冬不幸害死了自己的女儿，陷入了无尽的悲伤和自责中。神怜悯这位母亲，将她变成了能够飞翔的夜莺，可每个晚上她还是悲鸣着，思念自己的女儿。

知识拓展

画线双色单词或词汇为重点词汇

The Nightingale① and the Hawk②

A nightingale was perching③ in a tall tree and singing as usual when a hungry hawk swooped④ down and seized⑤ her. About to lose her life, the nightingale pleaded⑥ with the hawk to spare⑦ her life, saying she was too small to fill his stomach. If he were really hungry, she said, he should look for bigger birds. But the hawk replied, "Wouldn't I be a fool if I let go a meal already in my talons⑧ and go after something else which I haven't seen yet."

Only a fool would let go of something already in hands for unseen benefits.

词汇释义

① **nightingale**: /ˈnaɪtɪŋgeɪl/ *n.* 夜莺

② **hawk**: /hɔːk/ *n.* 鹰；隼

③ **perch**: /pɜːtʃ/ *v.* 栖息；停留

④ **swoop**: /swuːp/ *v.*（尤指为了袭击）向下猛冲，俯冲

⑤ **seize**: /siːz/ *v.* 抓住；捉住；夺

⑥ **plead**: /pliːd/ *v.* 乞求；恳求

⑦ **spare**: /speə/ *v.* 饶恕；赦免

⑧ **talon**: /ˈtælən/ *n.*（某些鸟类，尤指猛禽的）爪

本书标注的国际音标均为英式读音

1. 夜莺与鹰

在高高的大树上，一只**夜莺**像往常一样唱着歌。一只饥饿的**鹰**猛扑过去，一把将她抓住。临死之际，夜莺恳求鹰放过她，说自己个子太小，填不饱鹰的肚子。要是鹰觉得饿，应该找比她大的鸟来吃。鹰却回答："如果我放弃了早已到手的食物，而去追求还看不到的东西，那我不成傻瓜了吗？"

愚蠢的人才会为了贪图看不到的利益，而放弃已经到手的东西。

知识岛：希腊神话里的夜莺

◎ 在希腊神话中，底比斯王后埃冬不幸害死了自己的女儿，陷入了无尽的悲伤和自责中。神怜悯这位母亲，将她变成了能够飞翔的夜莺，可每个晚上她还是悲鸣着，思念自己的女儿。

The Nightingale[1] and the Hawk[2]

A nightingale was perching[3] in a tall tree and singing as usual when a hungry hawk swooped[4] down and seized[5] her. About to lose her life, the nightingale pleaded[6] with the hawk to spare[7] her life, saying she was too small to fill his stomach. "If he were really hungry," she said, "he should look for bigger birds." But the hawk replied, "Wouldn't I be a fool if I let go a meal already in my talons[8] and go after something else which I haven't seen yet."

Only a fool would let go of something already in hands for unseen benefits.

① **nightingale**: /ˈnaɪtɪŋgeɪl/ *n.* 夜莺

② **hawk**: /hɔːk/ *n.* 鹰；隼

③ **perch**: /pɜːtʃ/ *v.* 栖息；停留

④ **swoop**: /swuːp/ *v.*（尤指为了袭击）向下猛冲，俯冲

⑤ **seize**: /siːz/ *v.* 抓住；捉住；夺

⑥ **plead**: /pliːd/ *v.* 乞求；恳求

⑦ **spare**: /speə/ *v.* 饶恕；赦免

⑧ **talon**: /ˈtælən/ *n.*（某些鸟类，尤指猛禽的）爪

2. 猫与鸡

有只**猫**听说农场里有**鸡**生病了，就带着工具打扮成医生的模样去探望他们。一到农场，猫就迫不及待地询问鸡的病情。

鸡也立马回答："只要你离开这里，我们就好了。"

聪明的人能识破那些漂亮的谎言。

知识岛：埃及神话里的猫

◎ 在埃及神话中，死去的灵魂相伴着太阳神乘船在冥界行驶，途中会有巨蛇吸干河水，阻止太阳神前行。据说，此时会有猫现身斩下蛇头，守护太阳神一路安宁。

The Cat and the Chickens

A cat heard of some chickens on a farm that had taken ill, so he disguised[①] himself as a doctor to visit them with a medicine bag. As soon as he arrived at the farm, the cat eagerly asked how the chickens were feeling.

"We'll be fine," they replied, "once you get out of here."

The savvy can perceive[②] those beautiful lies.

① **disguise**: /dɪsˈgaɪz/ *v.* 假扮；伪装

② **perceive**: /pəˈsiːv/ *v.* 意识到；察觉，注意到

3. 山羊与牧羊人

一天，**牧羊人**吆喝着把羊群赶回羊圈，可一只馋嘴的**山羊**却不肯移动半步。牧羊人便生气地扔石头驱赶那只山羊，正巧石头砸断了他的一只羊角。牧羊人惊恐地恳求山羊不要把这件事告诉主人。山羊却回答："即便我不说，可我的角已经断了，这明摆着的事该怎么隐瞒呢？"

人们很难隐瞒明显的过错。

知识岛：希腊神话里的牧羊人

◎ 在希腊神话中，潘是一位掌管羊群与山林的牧神。他有着人的脑袋和上半身，长着羊角与羊腿。潘会随身带着排箫，一旦他开始吹奏就能催眠他人。

The Goat and the Goatherd[①]

One day, a goatherd was yelling and driving his goats back to their fold[②]. But a greedy goat stubbornly planted his hooves on the ground. The goatherd angrily threw a stone at him, breaking one of his horns[③]. In fright, the goatherd pleaded with the goat not to tell his master. But the goat replied, "Even if I were to keep mum, my horn is broken. How can I hide this obvious[④] thing?"

It is difficult to hide one´s blunders.

① **goatherd**: /ˈɡəʊthɜːd/ *n.* 牧羊人，羊倌

② **fold**: /fəʊld/ *n.* 羊圈，羊栏

③ **horn**: /hɔːn/ *n.*（羊、牛等动物的）角；（乐器）号

④ **obvious**: /ˈɒbviəs/ *adj.* 明显的；显然的

4. 山羊与驴

有人养了一只**山羊**和一头**驴**。驴的伙食总是很好，山羊就十分忌妒地对他说："你又是拉磨，又是背重东西，太辛苦了。不如装病摔倒，好好休息一下。"

驴听了山羊的话，摔得遍体鳞伤。于是他们的主人就请来医生为驴看病。医生说驴只要喝了用羊肺熬的汤就能痊愈。主人便立马将山羊杀了为驴治病。

算计别人可能会自食恶果。

The Goat and the Donkey

A man kept a goat and a donkey. The goat became jealous① of the donkey, because he was so well fed. So she said to him, "Life is hard for you to always turn the millstone② and carry the burdens. It's better to pretend③ to be sick so you can take a good rest."

The donkey followed her advice, fell down and was badly bruised④ all over. Their master sent for the vet⑤ and asked him for a remedy for these injuries. The vet told him that the donkey could recover only by drinking the soup made with goat's lungs⑥. As a result, the man sacrificed⑦ the goat to cure the donkey.

People whoever schemes⑧ against others owes his own misfortune⑨ to himself.

---

① **jealous**: /ˈdʒeləs/ *adj.* 吃醋的；忌妒的

② **millstone**: /ˈmɪlstəʊn/ *n.* 磨石；磨盘

③ **pretend**: /prɪˈtend/ *v.* 假装；佯装

④ **bruise**: /bruːz/ *v.* 撞伤；擦伤

⑤ **vet**: /vet/ *n.* 兽医；兽医诊所

⑥ **lung**: /lʌŋ/ *n.* 肺，肺部

⑦ **sacrifice**: /ˈsækrɪfaɪs/ *v.* 牺牲；献出

⑧ **scheme**: /skiːm/ *v.* 密谋；策划

⑨ **misfortune**: /ˌmɪsˈfɔːtʃuːn/ *n.* 厄运；不幸

5. 两只公鸡与鹰

两只**公鸡**为了争抢母鸡而打架。斗败的公鸡逃进了树丛里。得胜的公鸡则拍着翅膀，站在高高的墙上大声歌唱。

这时，一只**鹰**朝那只公鸡猛扑过来，一把将他抓走。而躲藏在树丛里的公鸡便拥有了母鸡。

骄傲与自满可能招来杀身之祸。

The Two Cocks and the Eagle[①]

Two cocks were fighting over some hens[②]. The defeated one withdrew[③] into a thicket[④]. The victor stood on the high wall, flapping[⑤] his wings and singing with a loud voice.

At this moment, an eagle swooped at him and carried him off. And from then on, the cock hidden in the thicket owned the hens.

Pride and complacency[⑥] go before a fall[⑦].

---

① **eagle**: /ˈiːgl/ *n.* 鹰

② **hen**: /hen/ *n.* 母鸡；雌禽

③ **withdraw**: /wɪðˈdrɔː/ *v.* 抽回；取回；提取；撤回，撤离

④ **thicket**: /ˈθɪkɪt/ *n.* 灌木丛；小树丛

⑤ **flap**: /flæp/ *v.* 振（翅）；（使上下或左右）拍打，摆动

⑥ **complacency**: /kəmˈpleɪsnsi/ *n.* 自满；自鸣得意

⑦ **fall**: /fɔːl/ *n.* 跌倒；降落；灭亡；失势

6. 渔夫与金枪鱼

渔夫们出海捕鱼，辛苦了一整天却一无所获。他们都垂头丧气地坐在船上。这时，一条被追赶的**金枪鱼**不小心跳进了渔夫们的船舱。渔夫们一把将这条大鱼抓住，在集市上卖了个好价钱。

有时靠技术得不到的，运气却可以成全你。

想一想

◎ 更好地完成一件事，除了运气和技术，还需要什么呢？

The Fishermen and the Tuna[①]

Some fishermen went fishing on the sea. They worked hard all day but caught nothing. They all sat dejectedly[②] on board. Just at that moment, a tuna, who was being chased[③], jumped accidentally into their boat. They seized the big fish and sold it at a good price in the market.

What skill denies us, chance may give us freely.

① **tuna**: /ˈtjuːnə/ *n.* 金枪鱼

② **dejectedly**: /dɪˈdʒektɪdli/ *adv.* 沮丧地；失望地

③ **chase**: /tʃeɪs/ *v.* 追赶，追逐；追捕

7. 捉到石头的渔夫

渔夫们拉起一张沉甸甸的渔网。大家都以为捕到了很多鱼，便高兴得手舞足蹈起来。可拉上岸的渔网里除了几条小鱼，全是些**石头**和瓦片。渔夫们觉得十分沮丧，刚才的欢喜一下化为泡影。

他们之中的一个老者便说道："朋友们，不要垂头丧气了，快乐和痛苦就像一对如影随形的孪生姐妹，刚才我们已经快乐过了，现在何不与痛苦相处一下？"

人生有起有落，就像晴朗的天空有时会突然出现风暴。千万不要因为一时的挫败而一蹶不振。

The Fishermen Who Caught Stones

Some fishermen were hauling① in a heavy dragnet②. As it was so heavy, they rejoiced and danced, imagining that they had caught a lot of fish. But when they dragged the net to the shore, they found it was full of stones and trash except a few small fish. The fishermen felt very frustrated③ with their dreams broken into pieces.

An old man among them said, "My friends, don't be depressed④. Happiness and pain are twin sisters that follow one another. We have been happy just now, why not get along with pain right now?"

Life has its ups and downs, just like a storm will suddenly appear on a sunny sky. Don't collapse⑤ after one setback⑥.

---

① **haul**: /hɔːl/ *v.* （用力）拉，拖（重物）

② **dragnet**: /ˈdræɡnet/ *n.* 拖网，拉网

③ **frustrated**: /frʌˈstreɪtɪd/ *adj.* 灰心的，气馁的

④ **depressed**: /dɪˈprest/ *adj.* 抑郁的；沮丧的；消沉的

⑤ **collapse**: /kəˈlæps/ *v.* （由于压力、无力或缺乏支持而）倒塌；垮掉

⑥ **setback**: /ˈsetbæk/ *n.* 挫折；阻碍

8. 渔夫与小鱼

渔夫捕了一天鱼，结果只捕到一条**小鱼**。那条小鱼恳求渔夫放了自己，说："我还太小，等我以后长成了大鱼，你再来抓我，这样你能得到更多好处。"

渔夫却回答："我可不管你以后能长多大，反正现在我已经抓住你了，把你放了，我就成傻瓜了。"

当下拥有的利益即使很小，也比幻想中的大。

The Fisherman and the Little Fish

A fisherman caught a single small fish as the result of his all day's labour. The little fish begged the fisherman to let him go. He said," I'm still too young. Catch me when I grow up and become a big fish, then you can make more profit[1] ."

"I'd be a fool to let you go when I've got you in my hand just in hope of better things to come, no matter how large you might become!" replied the fisherman.

A small gain is worth more than a large promise.

---

① **profit**: /ˈprɒfɪt/ *n.* 利润，赢利；好处

9. 翡翠鸟

翡翠鸟是一种喜欢独居的海鸟。传说为了躲避人们的捕杀，他们会在海边的岩壁上筑巢，然后生下自己的宝宝。有一回，一只翡翠鸟外出找食物，不料海上起了暴风雨，巨大的海浪将鸟巢卷进海中，翡翠鸟的宝宝们都淹死了。

翡翠鸟回来看到这一切，哀叹道：“我太不幸了。我为了躲避人类的捕杀藏身于海上，没想到这儿更不安全。”

没有一个地方绝对安全。

The Halcyon[①]

The halcyon is a kind of bird who loves solitude[②] and who lives constantly on the sea. It is said that to protect[③] themselves from human hunters, they would build their nests on the rocky cliffs of the coast[④], and give birth to their babies there. One day, when a halcyon was out in search of food, a storm came on the sea unexpectedly[⑤]. A huge wave swept the nest into the sea and all the young birds were drowned[⑥].

When the halcyon returned and saw what happened, she cried out, " How unfortunate[⑦]! I hid on the sea in order to avoid hunting and killing. I didn't expect it to be more insecure[⑧] here."

No place is truly safe.

---

① **halcyon**: /ˈhælsiən/ *n.* 翡翠鸟；传说中的幸福鸟

② **solitude**: /ˈsɒlɪtjuːd/ *n.* 独处；独居

③ **protect**: /prəˈtekt/ *v.* 保护；防护

④ **coast**: /kəʊst/ *n.* 海岸，沿海地区

⑤ **unexpectedly**: /ˌʌnɪkˈspektɪdli/ *adv.* 意外地；出乎意料地

⑥ **drown**: /draʊn/ *v.* （使）淹死，（使）溺死

⑦ **unfortunate**: /ʌnˈfɔːtʃnət/ *adj.* 不幸的，倒霉的

⑧ **insecure**: /ˌɪnsɪˈkjʊə/ *adj.* 不安全的；不牢靠的

10. 胀肚的狐狸

一只饥饿的**狐狸**发现了牧羊人藏在树洞里的面包和肉，便偷偷钻进树洞，把这些食物全吃了。可吃饱后，狐狸发现自己的肚子变得又大又圆，怎么也钻不出树洞，便在树洞里又哭又号。

这时，另一只狐狸路过树洞，听见了哀号。他走近树洞，问清了整件事情的经过，就对树洞里的狐狸说道："你不要着急，先暂时待在树洞里，等到身体恢复原样，就能轻轻松松钻出树洞了。"

有时，时间能解决许多困难的问题。

The Fox with a Swollen[①] Stomach

A starving[②] fox found inside a hole of a trunk some bread and meat hidden by a shepherd. He squeezed[③] into the hole and ate all the food. But his stomach became swollen so much that he could not get out. He began to cry and wail[④] in the hole.

At this moment, another fox passed by and heard him crying. He approached[⑤] to the hole and asked him about the whole thing, and then said to the fox, "Don't worry, you will have to remain there until you become such as you were when you crept in. Then you can get out easily enough."

Now and then, time resolves difficulties.

① **swollen**: /ˈswəʊlən/ *adj.* 肿胀的

② **starving**: /ˈstɑːvɪŋ/ *adj.* 极饿的；饥饿的

③ **squeeze**: /skwiːz/ *v.* 挤压；挤入；塞入

④ **wail**: /weɪl/ *v.* 恸哭；号啕

⑤ **approach**: /əˈprəʊtʃ/ *v.* （在距离或时间上）靠近，接近

11. 狐狸与刺藤

一只**狐狸**跳上篱笆，却不小心滑了一跤。眼看就要摔下去时，他赶忙抓住**刺藤**求助，可爪子却被刺藤扎得血流不止。狐狸对着刺藤叫唤道："哎呀，我原本指望你能救我，谁知道你把我害得更惨。"

刺藤回答："亲爱的朋友，你向我求助估计是找错了对象。你想依靠我，而我却是依靠别人的。"

千万不要依靠那些不能依靠的人。

想一想

◎ 一个值得依靠的人应该是什么样的？

The Fox and the Bramble[1]

A fox was mounting a hedge[2] when he slipped[3] and grabbed[4] a bramble to save himself. The thorns[5] of the bramble stuck into his paws[6] and made them bleed. Crying out in pain, the fox yelled, " Oh, I turned to you for help and now I am worse off!"

The bramble replied, " I'm afraid you've got it all wrong, dear friend. You tried to cling[7] to me, who am myself always catching at others."

Never rely on those who cannot be relied on.

---

① **bramble**: /ˈbræmbl/ *n.* 有刺灌木；刺藤

② **hedge**: /hedʒ/ *n.*（尤指花园、田地或马路边缘的）树篱

③ **slip**: /slɪp/ *v.* 滑倒；溜

④ **grab**: /ɡræb/ *v.* 抓住；攫取

⑤ **thorn**: /θɔːn/ *n.*（玫瑰之类植物的）刺，棘刺

⑥ **paw**: /pɔː/ *n.* 爪，爪子

⑦ **cling**: /klɪŋ/ *v.* 依附，附着；抓紧，抱紧

12. 狐狸与樵夫

一只**狐狸**在躲避猎人的途中遇见了一个**樵夫**。狐狸请求樵夫把自己藏起来。樵夫便把狐狸藏进了自己的小屋中。不一会儿，猎人们追来了，问樵夫有没有看到一只狐狸。樵夫虽然嘴上说没看到，却用手势暗示猎人们狐狸正躲在小屋里。然而猎人们只注意到樵夫的话，并没有留心樵夫的手势。

狐狸见猎人们走远后，就从小屋里跑出来，一声不吭地就要跑掉。樵夫责怪狐狸对救命恩人毫不感激。狐狸回答："如果你做的能和你说的一样，我就会真心感激你。"

有些人心口不一，当面说得好，背地里却干坏事。

The Fox and the Woodcutter[1]

A fox, running before the hunters, saw a woodcutter and begged him to hide him. The woodcutter hid him in his hut[2]. A few moments later, the hunters arrived and asked the woodcutter if he had seen a fox. The woodcutter replied that he had not seen him, but gave them a sign that he was right in the hut. The hunters, however, believing in his words, paid no attention to his gestures[3].

After they had gone, the fox ran out of the hut without saying anything. When the woodcutter reproached[4] him for showing no gratitude[5] for having saved him, the fox replied, " I would thank you if your behaviours are as kind as your words."

Some people talk like saints[6] but actually behave like rascals[7].

---

① **woodcutter**: /ˈwʊdkʌtə/ *n.* 樵夫

② **hut**: /hʌt/ *n.* 简陋的小房子（或棚、舍）

③ **gesture**: /ˈdʒestʃə/ *n.* 手势；姿势；示意动作；（表明感情或意图的）姿态，表示

④ **reproach**: /rɪˈprəʊtʃ/ *v.* 责备；责怪；指责；斥责

⑤ **gratitude**: /ˈɡrætɪtjuːd/ *n.* 感激之情；感谢

⑥ **saint**: /seɪnt/ *n.* 圣人

⑦ **rascal**: /ˈrɑːskl/ *n.* 无赖；流氓；恶棍

13. 狐狸与豹子

狐狸与**豹子**比美。豹子不断炫耀自己身上漂亮的斑点。狐狸却说："我可比你美多了。我不仅有好看的外表，还有更美的心灵。"

智识的装饰胜于身体之美。

The Fox and the Leopard[①]

A fox and a leopard were having a beauty contest[②]. The leopard boasted[③] constantly about the various spots that decorated[④] his body.

The fox replied, " I'm much more beautiful than you, for I am decorated, not only in body, but also in mind[⑤]."

A beautiful mind is more attractive[⑥] than a pretty appearance[⑦].

---

① **leopard**: /ˈlepəd/ *n.* 豹

② **contest**: /ˈkɒntest/ *n.* 比赛；竞赛

③ **boast**: /bəʊst/ *v.* 自夸；自吹自擂

④ **decorate**: /ˈdekəreɪt/ *v.* 装饰，装点，打扮

⑤ **mind**: /maɪnd/ *n.* 头脑；大脑

⑥ **attractive**: /əˈtræktɪv/ *adj.* 吸引人的；有魅力的

⑦ **appearance**: /əˈpɪərns/ *n.* 外貌；外表

14. 狐狸与被选为王的猴子

猴子在野兽的聚会上表演跳舞，受到热烈欢迎，被大家推举为王。**狐狸**因此非常忌妒，他把一个放着肉的捕兽夹说成一个要献给猴子的宝物。猴子想也没想，就跟着狐狸走近那个捕兽夹。落入陷阱的猴子责备狐狸陷害自己，狐狸却说：“像你这样的大傻瓜，还想当百兽之王？”

做事轻佻的人会给自己招来不幸与嘲笑。

想一想

◎ 你觉得猴子适合当百兽之王吗？百兽之王该是什么样子呢？

The Fox and the Monkey Elected King

A monkey once danced in an assembly of the beasts. So pleased by his performance① that they elected him their king. A fox, envying him so much, said to the monkey he wanted to present him a treasure②, which actually a trap③ with meat on it. The monkey approached carelessly and was caught in the trap. The monkey blamed the fox for cheating him, but the fox replied, " How can a fool like you become the king of the beasts? "

People who act frivolously④ will incur⑤ misfortune and ridicule⑥ to themselves.

---

① **performance**: /pəˈfɔːməns/ *n.* 表演；演出

② **treasure**: /ˈtreʒə/ *n.* 宝物；财宝

③ **trap**: /træp/ *n.*（捕捉动物的）陷阱，夹，捕捉器

④ **frivolously**: /ˈfrɪvləsli/ *adv.* 轻浮地；愚昧地

⑤ **incur**: /ɪnˈkɜː/ *v.* 招致；遭受；引起；引致，带来（成本、花费等）

⑥ **ridicule**: /ˈrɪdɪkjuːl/ *n.* 讥笑；嘲笑

15. 断了尾巴的狐狸

有只**狐狸**被捕兽器夹断了尾巴。他感到非常羞耻，就决定劝说其他狐狸也去掉尾巴。如果大家都一样了，他的缺点也就不会被人发现了。于是他喊来了所有狐狸，劝他们割去丑陋又笨重的尾巴。

这时，有一只狐狸站起来说道："喂，朋友，如果不会对你有利，你是绝对不会这样劝我们的。"

有些人给你劝告并非出于好意，而是为了他自己的利益。

The Fox with the Cropped[1] Tail

A fox, having had his tail cut by a trap, was so ashamed[2] that he resolved to induce[3] other foxes to cut their tails. If they all had no tails, the defect of his would not be noticed. Thus, he called a meeting of all the foxes and recommended[4] them to cut off their heavy and ugly tails.

Then one of the foxes stood up and said, " Hey, friend! If it had not been to your own advantage[5], you wouldn't have given us this advice!"

Some people give advice not out of kindness but for their own interests.

---

① **crop**: /krɒp/ *v.* 剪短；修剪

② **ashamed**: /əˈʃeɪmd/ *adj.* 羞愧的；不好意思的，难为情的

③ **induce**: /ɪnˈdjuːs/ *v.* 诱使；劝说

④ **recommend**: /ˌrekəˈmend/ *v.* 推荐；建议

⑤ **advantage**: /ədˈvɑːntɪdʒ/ *n.* 有利条件；优势；好处

16. 没见过狮子的狐狸

一只**狐狸**从来没有见过**狮子**。一次偶然的机会，他在森林里遇到了狮子，被吓得半死。当他第二次遇到狮子时，仍很惧怕，但比起第一次好多了。第三次遇到狮子时，他竟有勇气走上前去，与狮子聊起天来。

不要惧怕不熟悉的事物，接近它，你就会发现没什么可怕的。

The Fox Who Had Never Seen a Lion

A fox had never seen a lion before. One day he happened to meet one face to face. He was terribly frightened.[①] The second time he saw the lion he was also frightened, but not so much as the first time. But the third time, he had the courage[②] to approach him and began to talk to him.

Don't be afraid of unfamiliar[③] things. You will find that there's nothing scary[④] when you approach it.

---

① **frightened**: /ˈfraɪtnd/ *adj.* 惊吓的；害怕的

② **courage**: /ˈkʌrɪdʒ/ *n.* 勇气；勇敢

③ **unfamiliar**: /ˌʌnfəˈmɪliə/ *adj.* 不熟悉的

④ **scary**: /ˈskeəri/ *adj.* 恐怖的；吓人的

17. 凭空许愿的穷人

有一个**穷人**生了很严重的病。医生们也觉得没有治好的希望了。穷人便向神明许愿，如果自己能够康复，便会向神明献上一百头牛。

一旁的妻子就问穷人："你到哪去弄这些买牛的钱呢？"

穷人回答："你以为神明治好了我的病，真会向我索要这些东西吗？"

人们容易许诺自己做不到的事情。

想一想

◎ 为了完成一件事，除了许愿，我们还能做些什么呢？

The Poor Man Who Promised[1] the Impossible

There was a poor man who had a serious[2] illness. The doctors also felt that there was no cure for the disease. So he made a wish to the gods that if he could recover[3], he would offer one hundred cows to the gods.

His wife at his side asked him, "Where are you going to get the money to buy those cows?"

The poor man replied, "Do you think gods might ask me for these things for curing me?"

People readily[4] make promises which they have no intention[5] of keeping.

---

① **promise**: /ˈprɒmɪs/ *v.* 允诺，答应；保证

② **serious**: /ˈsɪəriəs/ *adj.* 严重的；糟糕的；严肃的，认真的

③ **recover**: /rɪˈkʌvə/ *v.* （在疾病或受伤之后）完全恢复健康

④ **readily**: /ˈredɪli/ *adv.* 迅速地；轻而易举地；心甘情愿地

⑤ **intention**: /ɪnˈtenʃn/ *n.* 意图，意向；目的，打算

18. 赫耳墨斯与被蚂蚁咬了的人

一天，一个**人**看见一艘船遇难了，船上的乘客都被淹死了。他便抱怨神明做事不公，为了处死船上的一个坏人，却让其他无辜的人一起遇难。

在他说这话时，一群**蚂蚁**围在了他的脚边，有只蚂蚁咬了他一口。为了除掉那只蚂蚁，他把所有的蚂蚁都踩死了。

突然，**赫耳墨斯**出现在他面前，一边用权杖敲他，一边说道："这下你该明白，你和神明都会做出同样的事。"

人不应苛求别人，因为自己有时也会犯同别人一样的错误。

知识岛：赫耳墨斯

◎ 赫耳墨斯是希腊神话中众神的使者，他常常戴着一顶插着翅膀的帽子，穿着一双有翅膀的凉鞋，手里握着一根缠着两条蛇的权杖，给人间送去宙斯的神谕。传说他还是个发明家，发明了字母、里拉琴，还有体育运动。

Hermes[1] and the Man Bitten by an Ant

One day, a man saw a ship sink[2] with all its passengers. Then he claimed[3] it was unfair for gods to kill one evil man and let the innocent[4] people die together.

As he was saying this, a cluster of ants gathered around his feet. Then one of them bit him. In order to kill it, he crushed[5] them all.

Then Hermes appeared to him, and struck him with his wand, saying, "Now you understand that gods and you may act in the same way."

Don't be hard[6] on others, because sometimes you make the same mistakes as them.

---

① **Hermes**: /ˈhəːmiːz/ *n.* 赫耳墨斯（希腊神话中众神的使者，亡灵的接引神。司掌商业、交通、畜牧、竞技等，也是盗贼和旅者的保护神）

② **sink**: /sɪŋk/ *v.* （使）沉没；（使）陷入；沉下

③ **claim**: /kleɪm/ *v.* 宣称；声称

④ **innocent**: /ˈɪnəsnt/ *adj.* 无辜的；清白的

⑤ **crush**: /krʌʃ/ *v.* 压碎；捣碎；碾成粉末

⑥ **hard**: /hɑːd/ *adj.* 严厉的，苛刻的

19. 男人与他的妻子

有个**男人**有一个**妻子**，她与家中的所有人都难以相处。丈夫很想知道她与她娘家的人是否也是如此，于是便找了一个借口把她送回了娘家。过了几天，他的妻子回来了。丈夫问妻子她娘家的人待她如何。妻子回答说："那些放牛的与放羊的都不给我好脸色看。"于是丈夫对妻子说："啊，亲爱的，若那些早出晚归的用人都不喜欢你，那么你还能指望那些整天与你待在一起的人能好好对待你吗？"

一件事常常可以由小见大。

The Man and His Wife

A man had a wife who had trouble getting along with everyone in the family. The husband wanted to know if she behaved① the same way in her father's home. So he made some excuse② to send her home on a visit to her father. After a short time the wife returned. The man asked her how her family treated her. The wife replied, " I could see aversion③ on the faces of those shepherds." So the husband said to her, "Ah, my dear, if those who go out early in the morning and return late in the evening do not like you, how can you expect those who stay with you all day to treat you well?"

A straw will show which way the wind blows.

---

① **behave**: /bɪˈheɪv/ *v.*（以某种方式）行事，表现

② **excuse**: /ɪkˈskjuːz/ *n.* 理由，借口

③ **aversion**: /əˈvəːʃn/ *n.* 厌恶，反感

20. 吹牛的运动员

有个**运动员**总是在参加比赛的时候缺乏勇气。人们都在指责他，于是他决定远走他乡。过了些时日，他回来了，逢人就说自己在别的城市参加了很多比赛，拿了很多名次，尤其是他在罗德岛参加跳远比赛，创造了连奥林匹克冠军都无法超越的成绩。他还说，如果当时那些在场的人能来到这里，就可以为他作证。

这时，人群中有人对他说："喂，朋友，如果这一切是真的，那根本不需要什么证人。你就把这里当作是罗德岛，现在就跳给我们看吧！"

不能用事实证明的事，说再多都没有意义。

知识岛：奥林匹斯山

◎ 古希腊人认为奥林匹斯山是光汇聚的地方，也是神明们居住的乐园。他们在那里载歌载舞，还举行各种运动比赛。

The Boasting Athlete[1]

There was an athlete who always lacked courage when participating[2] in competitions[3]. Accused by others, he decided to go on a long journey[4]. Some time later, he came back and told everyone that he had participated in many competitions in other cities and won many prizes. Especially in the long jump competition on Rhodes, where he created a record that even an Olympic champion[6] could not break. He also said that if those present at the time could come here, they would prove[7] it.

At that moment, someone in the crowd said to him, "Now, my friend, if all this is true, there is no need of witnesses at all. Suppose[8] this is Rhodes, and jump for us."

Facts speak louder than words.

---

① **athlete**: /ˈæθliːt/ *n.* 运动员；田径运动员

② **participate**: /pɑːˈtɪsɪpeɪt/ *v.* 参加；参与

③ **competition**: /ˌkɒmpəˈtɪʃn/ *n.* 竞争；比赛

④ **journey**: /ˈdʒɜːni/ *n.* （尤指长途）旅行，行程

⑤ **Rhodes**: /ˈrəʊdz/ *n.* （希腊）罗德岛

⑥ **champion**: /ˈtʃæmpiən/ *n.* 冠军

⑦ **prove**: /pruːv/ *v.* 证明；证实

⑧ **suppose**: /səˈpəʊz/ *conj.* 假如；假设

21. 烧炭的与漂布的

烧炭的在一间房子里做生意，看见一个**漂布的**也想在附近开店。他便走过去劝漂布的和自己同住，好节省店租。

漂布的听完，赶紧摇摇头说：“这可使不得，我好不容易洗干净的东西，都会被你的煤烟染黑的。”

物以类聚，人以群分。

The Charcoal-Burner[1] and the Fuller[2]

A charcoal-burner carried on his trade in a house. One day he met a fuller who wanted to come and settle in the same neighbourhood. He invited the fuller to come and stay with him, saying that the rent could be lessened.

Hearing his words, the fuller shook his head and replied, "The arrangement[3] is impossible as far as I am concerned[4], for whatever I should whiten may immediately be blackened by your charcoal."

Birds of a feather flock together.

---

① **charcoal-burner**: /ˈtʃɑːkəʊl ˈbɜːnə/ *n.* 烧炭者

② **fuller**: /ˈfʊlə/ *n.* 漂洗工

③ **arrangement**: /əˈreɪndʒmənt/ *n.* 安排；筹备

④ **concern**: /kənˈsɜːn/ *v.* 与……有关；涉及

22. 人与宙斯

传说创世之初，**宙斯**先创造了动物，并分别赐给不同的动物力量、速度和一对翅膀。之后，**人**赤裸裸地出生了。人问宙斯："您不打算赐给我点什么吗？"

宙斯说道："难道你没有感受到我赐予你的语言和思想？它们使你同神一样强大，鸟兽的力量再大，速度再快，都只能甘拜下风。"

人领悟地点点头，怀着对宙斯的敬畏与感激，开始了生命的旅程。

语言和思想是人类最宝贵的财富。

想一想

◎ 父母给你最大的礼物又是什么呢？

Man and Zeus[1]

Legend has it that when the world was created, Zeus first created animals and gave them strength[2], speed and wings respectively. After that, man was born naked. Man asked Zeus, "Aren't you going to give me some gift?"

Zeus said, "Don't you feel the speech and the ability to reason I gave to you? These make you as powerful as gods. No matter how powerful the birds and beasts are, no matter how fast they are, they can only bow down and admit defeat[3]."

Man, recognizing his gifts, nodded and began the journey of life with awe and gratitude for Zeus.

Speech and rational mind are the greatest gifts given to mankind.

---

① **Zeus**: /zjuːs/ *n.* 宙斯，希腊神话中的众神之王

② **strength**: /streŋθ/ *n.* 体力；力量；力气；实力

③ **defeat**: /dɪˈfiːt/ *n.* 失败；战败

23. 农夫与狐狸

有个**农夫**常常受到**狐狸**的骚扰，于是想狠狠地教训一下狐狸。他抓住狐狸，把浸过油的绳子绑在狐狸的尾巴上，然后点着火。可尾巴着火的狐狸却跑到了那人辛苦耕种的田地里。当时正是收获的季节，那人一边追赶着狐狸，一边为自己被烧毁的庄稼而痛苦。

极度的愤怒会让人失去理智，从而招来更大的灾祸。

The Farmer and the Fox

A farmer was greatly annoyed① by a fox, so he determined to take a revenge. He caught the fox and tied a rope② soaked③ in oil to his tail, then set it on fire. But the fox with its tail on fire ran into the field where the man had worked hard and cultivated④. It was the harvest⑤ season. The man ran after the fox, lamenting⑥ his lost crops⑦.

Extreme⑧ anger can make people lose their minds and bring on greater disasters⑨.

---

① **annoy**: /əˈnɔɪ/ *v.* 使恼怒；打扰

② **rope**: /rəʊp/ *n.* 线缆；绳索

③ **soak**: /səʊk/ *v.* 浸泡；浸湿

④ **cultivate**: /ˈkʌltɪveɪt/ *v.* 耕作；培育

⑤ **harvest**: /ˈhɑːvɪst/ *n.* 收获；收成

⑥ **lament**: /ləˈment/ *v.* 对……感到悲痛，痛惜

⑦ **crop**: /krɒp/ *n.* 庄稼，作物；收成

⑧ **extreme**: /ɪkˈstriːm/ *adj.* 极度的；极大的

⑨ **disaster**: /dɪˈzɑːstə/ *n.* 灾难，大祸

24. 人与狮子

有一回，**人**与**狮子**一同旅行。一路上，他们各自夸奖自己。这时他们经过一座石像，展现了一个人击败了一头狮子。

人便指着石像说：“你看，我们比狮子强吧。”

狮子微笑着说道：“假如狮子会雕刻，那么你会看到很多人被踩在狮子的脚下。”

立场不同，得出的结论就会不同。

The Man and the Lion

Once upon a time, a man and a lion were companions[①] on a journey. On the way, they began to boast about their prowess[②]. Then they passed a statue[③] carved[④] in stone, which depicted[⑤] a lion defeated by a man.

The man pointed to it and said, " There, we are much stronger than lions!"

The lion smiled and replied, " If we lions knew how to carve, you would see many people under the paws of lions."

People with different points of view[⑥] tell different stories.

---

① **companion**: /kəmˈpæniən/ *n.* 旅伴；伴侣

② **prowess**: /ˈpraʊes/ *n.* 杰出的才能，高超的技能

③ **statue**: /ˈstætʃuː/ *n.* 雕像，雕塑，塑像

④ **carve**: /kɑːv/ *v.* 雕刻；刻

⑤ **depict**: /dɪˈpɪkt/ *v.* 描绘，描述

⑥ **view**: /vjuː/ *n.* 观点；看法；视野

25. 人与萨特尔

从前，有**人**在森林里结识了**萨特尔**，并同他成为好朋友。冬天到了，天气变得非常寒冷，那人就把手放到嘴边呵气。萨特尔问他为什么这样做。那人回答，这样可以取暖。

后来，他们又一起吃饭。食物很烫，那人就把食物夹到嘴边吹气。萨特尔问他这又是做什么。那人回答说那肉太烫，这样可以吹凉。

萨特尔对那人说道："喂，朋友！我只好同你绝交了，因为从你的嘴里既可以出热气又可以出冷风。"

千万不可与那些反复无常的人交朋友。

知识岛：萨特尔

◎ 萨特尔是希腊神话中一种生活在山林间的半人半兽神。他的上半身似人，下半身似羊，有着蓬松的头发和尖尖的耳朵，样貌与牧神潘颇为相像。

The Man and the Satyr[①]

A man once met a Satyr in the forest, and made friends with him. When winter came, it became very cold. The man put his hands to his mouth and blew on them. The Satyr asked him why he did that. The man replied that he did it to warm his hands.

Later, they ate together. The food was very hot, so the man put the food to his mouth and blew. The Satyr asked him again what he was doing. The man replied that the meat was too hot, it could let it cool.

The Satyr said to the man, "Hey, friend! I can no longer consider you as a friend, because you can blow both hot and cold air from your mouth."

We must never make friends with those who are capricious[②].

① **Satyr**: /ˈsætə/ n. 萨特尔，希腊神话中的半人半兽神

② **capricious**: /kəˈprɪʃəs/ *adj.* 反复无常的

26. 农夫与狼

农夫帮牛解下犁，牵着它去喝水。这时，有只饿肚子的**狼**正好出来找食物。狼朝犁走过去，开始舔轭的内侧，感觉仿佛尝到了牛肉的香味。狼就这样不知不觉地一点一点将头伸进了轭中，然后被卡住了。他想挣脱，竟然拉着犁在田里走来走去，仿佛在耕地似的。

农夫回来后，看见眼前的景象说道："可恶的坏东西！但愿你从今往后不要再作恶，乖乖种地吧。"

尽管有些恶人做了一点善事，那也并非他的本意，而是出于无奈。

The Farmer and the Wolf

A farmer loosed his ox from the plough[1] and led it away to drink water. While he was absent[2], a hungry wolf came out looking for food. The wolf went to the plough, and began to lick the inner side of the yoke[3], savouring the taste of beef. Bit by bit, the wolf unknowingly put his head into the yoke, and was stuck[4] there. Unable to free himself, the wolf dragged the plough in the field as if he was ploughing.

The farmer came back. Seeing what was happening, he said, "You devil rascal! I wish you would stop being wicked[5] from now on and do farm work instead."

Even though some wicked people did some good deeds[6], it was not by choice, but because of helplessness.

---

① **plough**: /plaʊ/ *n.* 犁；*v.* 犁地，耕地

② **absent**: /ˈæbsənt/ *adj.* 缺席；不在

③ **yoke**: /jəʊk/ *n.* 轭；（尤指）牛轭

④ **stuck**: /stʌk/ *adj.* 卡住；陷住

⑤ **wicked**: /ˈwɪkɪd/ *adj.* 邪恶的；缺德的

⑥ **deed**: /diːd/ *n.* 行为；行动

27. 天文学家

有个**天文学家**每个晚上都要外出观察星星。一天深夜，他来到郊外，目不转睛地看着天上的星星，一不小心掉进了一口枯井中。天文学家大喊起来，有人路过听到了他的呼救，问清了事情的经过，便对天文学家说："喂，朋友，你只留心天上的东西，却不肯弄清地上的事吗？"

不要因为一心想做大事，就忽略了身边的小事。有时导致失败的，正是这些不起眼的小事。

知识岛：天文学家张衡

◎ 张衡是中国东汉时期伟大的天文学家。他发明了浑天仪与地动仪。张衡是浑天说的代表人物，他认为地球漂浮于水上，日月星辰在天空中运行。

The Astronomer[1]

There was once an astronomer who used to go out at night to observe[2] the stars. One evening, as he was walking about outside the town, gazing[3] up into the sky, he fell into a dry well. As he called out for help, someone passing by heard him. Learning what had happened, the man said to the astronomer, " Hey, my friend, you only pay attention[4] to the things in the sky, do you not care what is on earth?"

It is always those trivial matters that matter.

---

① **astronomer**: /əˈstrɒnəmə/ *n.* 天文学家

② **observe**: /əbˈzɜːv/ *v.* 观察；观测

③ **gaze**: /ɡeɪz/ *v.* 凝视；注视

④ **attention**: /əˈtenʃn/ *n.* 注意；注意力

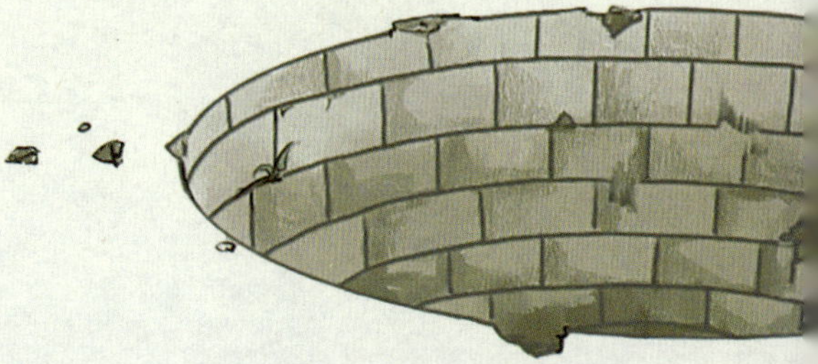

28. 青蛙邻居

两只**青蛙**是邻居。一只住在远离马路的池塘里，另一只住在马路上的水洼中。住在池塘里的青蛙常常劝马路上的青蛙搬到更安全的池塘来与自己同住，可马路上的青蛙说已经习惯了自己的水洼，不肯搬家。结果，他被路过的车子轧死了。

明知不好却不去改变，最终要承担由此造成的后果。

The Two Frogs as Neighbours

Two frogs were neighbours. One lived in a pond[①] far from the road, while the other lived in a puddle[②] on the road. The frog in the pond often advised the one on the road to move in and live with him. But the other frog refused[③], saying that he felt it so very hard to leave a place which he had become accustomed[④] to. As a result, he was crushed to death by a passing car.

Not correcting the mistake, one will have his way to his own hurt.

---

① **pond**: /pɒnd/ *n.* 池塘

② **puddle**: /ˈpʌdl/ *n.* 水洼；小水坑

③ **refuse**: /rɪˈfjuːz/ *v.* 拒绝；回绝；推却

④ **accustom**: /əˈkʌstəm/ *v.* 使习惯（于）；使适应

29. 池塘里的青蛙

两只**青蛙**住在池塘里。夏天到了，池塘干涸了，他们便开始寻找新的住所。他们路过一口很深的井，一只青蛙便对另一只青蛙说道：“喂，朋友，让我们一起去这井里住吧。”另一只青蛙回答：“可等这里的水也干了的时候，我们该怎么爬上来呢？”

三思而后行。

The Frogs in the Pond

Two frogs lived together in a pond. When the summer came, the pond dried up, so they left it to look for another place to live in. When they passed a deep well, one frog said to the other, " Hey, my friend, let's jump in and live here." The other replied, " Suppose this well dries up like the pond, how can we get out?"

Think twice before you act.

30. 三只公牛与狮子

三只公牛总是待在一起。有只**狮子**想要吃掉他们，可总是无法打败团结在一起的他们。于是狮子挑拨三只公牛，让他们产生矛盾。等到他们大吵一架，各自分开后，狮子就将公牛一个一个地吃掉了。

要善于分辨是非，不要听信谗言，当心被人挑拨离间。

想一想

◎ 你猜猜狮子都对公牛说了什么？

The Three Bulls and the Lion

Three bulls always stayed together. A lion intended[①] to eat them, but he couldn't defeat them when they stayed together. So he began to play them against[②] each other. When disagreements arose among them, they had a huge fight and finally separated. Then the lion ate the three bulls one by one.

Slanderous[③] talk may blur right and wrong and make mischief[④].

---

① **intend**: /ɪnˈtend/ *v.* 打算；意图

② **play sb./sth. against sb./sth.**：挑拨离间

③ **slanderous**: /ˈslɑːndrəs/ *adj.* 诋毁的

④ **make mischief**: 搬弄是非，挑拨离间

31. 金丝雀与蝙蝠

挂在窗口笼子里的**金丝雀**在夜晚唱着歌。一只**蝙蝠**听到后，飞来问金丝雀为什么在白天闷声不响，却在夜里歌唱。金丝雀回答，因为自己是在白天唱歌时被捉住的，从那以后她在白天就非常谨慎。蝙蝠却说："你现在才开始谨慎已经没用了，你应该在被捉住之前就懂得这个道理。"

事后预防，于事无补。

The Canary[1] and the Bat[2]

A canary, confined[3] in a cage hung outside a window, always sang at night. One night, a bat came and asked the canary why she was silent in the daytime and sang only at night. The canary replied that she was caught singing in the daytime, so since then she had been very cautious[4] during the daytime. Then the bat said, " It is no use you doing that now when you are a prisoner[5]. You should have known that before you were caught."

Precautions[6] are useless after the event.

① **canary**: /kəˈneəri/ *n.* 金丝雀

② **bat**: /bæt/ *n.* 蝙蝠

③ **confine**: /kənˈfaɪn/ *v.* 限制；监禁

④ **cautious**: /ˈkɔːʃəs/ *adj.* 小心的；谨慎的

⑤ **prisoner**: /ˈprɪznə/ *n.* 囚犯；犯人

⑥ **precaution**: /prɪˈkɔːʃn/ *n.* 预防，预防措施

32. 农夫与鹰

农夫发现一只美丽的鹰落入了猎人的捕兽夹，便救了那只鹰。鹰很感激，记下了这份恩情。有一天，鹰看到农夫坐在一堵快要倒塌的墙下，便立刻飞去抓起农夫的头巾。农夫刚一站起来追赶鹰，那墙就轰的一声倒下了。鹰的报恩令农夫十分感动。

做好事会得到回报。

The Farmer and the Eagle

A farmer found a beautiful eagle captured in a trap, and set him free. The eagle was grateful for his kindness. One day, he saw the farmer sitting under a wall which was about to collapse. He flew toward him and with his talons snatched[①] his kerchief[②]. No sooner had the farmer risen to chase the eagle than the wall under which he had been sitting fell down to pieces. He was very touched by the way the eagle returned his kindness .

Good deeds will be rewarded.

---

① **snatch**: /snætʃ/ *v.* 夺去；抢走

② **kerchief**: /ˈkəːtʃɪf/ *n.* 方头巾，方围巾

33. 农夫与狗

农夫被暴风雪困在家中，无法出门寻找食物，他只能吃掉自己的绵羊。可是风雪越来越大，之后，他又吃掉了耕田的牛。

农夫家的**狗**看到这一切，相互说道：“我们得赶紧离开了，主人把同他一起辛勤工作的牛都宰了，又怎么会放过我们呢？”

要警惕那些对家人都十分残忍的人。

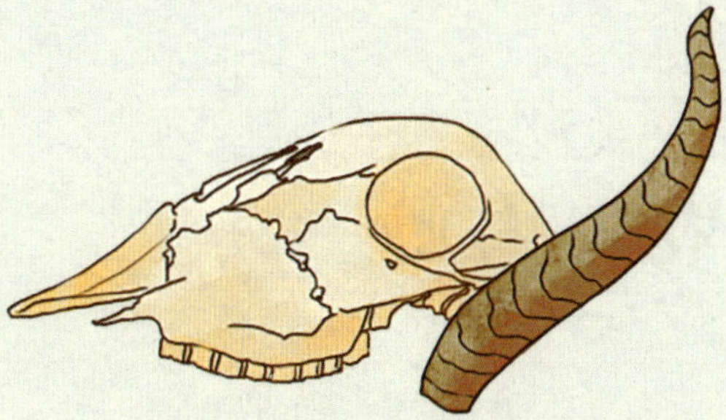

The Farmer and His Dogs

A farmer, snowed up① in his farmstead② by a severe③ storm, was unable to go out and get food. So he killed and ate his sheep. Then, as the storm continued, he was compelled④ to kill his oxen and eat them too.

On seeing this, his dogs said to one another, "We had better get out of here. The master even killed all his oxen who had worked hard with him. How could he spare us?"

Be wary⑤ of those who are very cruel⑥ to their family members.

---

① **be snowed up**: 因大雪而被困在某处

② **farmstead**: /ˈfɑːmsted/ *n.* 农舍及附近建筑物

③ **severe**: /sɪˈvɪə/ *adj.* 非常严重的；剧烈的；惨重的

④ **compel**: /kəmˈpel/ *v.* 强迫；迫使

⑤ **wary**: /ˈweəri/ *adj.* 谨慎的；小心

⑥ **cruel**: /ˈkruːəl/ *adj.* 残酷的；冷酷的

34. 农夫与蛇

农夫在雪地里发现了一条冻僵的**蛇**。农夫可怜他，把蛇放在自己的怀里。不久，蛇苏醒过来，却咬了农夫一口。

奄奄一息的农夫悲叹道："我真是该死，怎么可以怜惜坏人呢？"

即使帮助了坏人，也不能改变他们的本性。

想一想

◎ 什么样的人能被我们称为坏人？什么样的人能被我们认作好人？

The Farmer and the Snake[1]

A farmer found a frozen snake in the snow. Out of sympathy[2] he picked him up and placed him in his chest. The snake was quickly revived by the warmth and gave the farmer a fatal[3] bite.

As the poor man lay dying, he sighed, " I have just got what I deserved[4]. How could I take compassion[5] on so villainous[6] a creature[7]?"

Even if we help evildoers[8], we cannot change their nature.

---

① **snake**: /sneɪk/ *n.* 蛇

② **sympathy**: /ˈsɪmpəθi/ *n.* 同情

③ **fatal**: /ˈfeɪtl/ *adj.* 致命的

④ **deserve**: /dɪˈzɜːv/ *v.* 值得；应得

⑤ **compassion**: /kəmˈpæʃn/ *n.* 同情；怜悯

⑥ **villainous**: /ˈvɪlənəs/ *adj.* 邪恶的；极坏的

⑦ **creature**: /ˈkriːtʃə/ *n.* 生物；动物

⑧ **evildoer**: /ˈiːvəlˌduːə/ *n.* 歹徒；作恶的人

35. 农夫与他的儿子们

有个**农夫**在临终前想教会自己的**儿子们**耕种。他把儿子们叫到自己床边说："孩子们，我将离开这个世界了，你们可以去找我埋在葡萄园里的东西，这些东西会让你们衣食无忧。"

儿子们都以为父亲在葡萄园里埋了金银财宝。可他们把葡萄园翻了个底朝天，什么宝物也没找到。葡萄园却因此被好好耕作了一番，比以往结出了更多葡萄。

勤劳是人类最好的宝物。

The Farmer and His Sons

A dying farmer wanted to teach his sons how to farm. So he called them to his bedside and said, " My children, I am about to die. In my vineyard[①] I buried[②] something that will make you properly[③] fed and clothed."

His sons thought their father had buried treasures in the vineyard. So they turned up the soil[④] in the vineyard over and over again, but found nothing. However, after such a thorough digging, the vines repaid their labour by an extraordinary crop.

Hard work is the best treasure of mankind.

---

① **vineyard**: /ˈvɪnjɑːd/ *n.* 葡萄园

② **bury**: /ˈberi/ *v.* 埋；埋葬

③ **properly**: /ˈprɒpəli/ *adv.* 正确地；适当地

④ **soil**: /sɔɪl/ *n.* 土壤

36. 农夫与苹果树

农夫的田里长着一棵**苹果树**，这棵树结不出苹果，却住着好些麻雀和吵闹的蝉。农夫觉得这树没什么用处，决定将它砍掉。他刚拿起斧子，朝树砍了一下，那些蝉和麻雀就恳求农夫不要砍倒他们的家，他们会在树上为农夫歌唱，让农夫快乐。

农夫没理睬，又砍了好几下，直至树上出现了一个大洞。这时，他发现树洞里竟然有蜂巢。他尝了尝蜂巢里的蜜，连忙抛下斧头，从此将那棵树小心地保护起来。

有些人做事只考虑自己的利益。

The Farmer and the Apple Tree

A farmer had an apple tree growing in his garden, which bore no fruit but merely[1] served as a shelter for some sparrows[2] and noisy cicadas[3]. Disappointed[4] at its barrenness[5], he determined to cut it down. As he picked up the axe and slashed[6] at the tree, the sparrows and cicadas begged him to spare the tree, saying that they will sing to him and make him happy.

The farmer, however, refused to listen to them, and slashed again on the trunk[7]. After a few strokes[8] he saw a hollow[9] which contained[10] a honeycomb[11]. After tasting the honey, he threw down his axe and took great care of the tree thereafter.

Some people would forsake[12] good for the sake of gold.

---

① **merely**: /ˈmɪəli/ *adv.* 仅仅；只不过
② **sparrow**: /ˈspærəʊ/ *n.* 麻雀
③ **cicada**: /sɪˈkɑːdə/ *n.* 蝉；知了
④ **disappointed**: /ˌdɪsəˈpɔɪntɪd/ *adj.* 失望的，沮丧的
⑤ **barrenness**: /ˈbærnnəs/ *n.* 贫瘠；不结果实
⑥ **slash**: /slæʃ/ *v.* （用利器）砍，劈
⑦ **trunk**: /trʌŋk/ *n.* 树干；象鼻
⑧ **stroke**: /strəʊk/ *n.* 击球（动作）；（打、击等的）一下，一击
⑨ **hollow**: /ˈhɒləʊ/ *n.* 凹陷处；洞
⑩ **contain**: /kənˈteɪn/ *v.* 包含；容纳
⑪ **honeycomb**: /ˈhʌnikəʊm/ *n.* 蜂巢
⑫ **forsake**: /fɔːˈseɪk/ *v.* 抛弃；摒弃

37. 农夫与争吵的儿子们

农夫的**儿子们**总是争吵不休，不论农夫训斥还是劝说都没什么用，于是农夫决定用事实教育教育他们。他让儿子们找来一捆木棍，然后让他们一个一个试着把这捆木棍折断。他的儿子们一个个用尽全力也没办法做到。接着，农夫解开那捆木棍，给了他们一人一根。这次，他们毫不费力地就将手里的木棍折断了。

这时，农夫说道："孩子们，你们就像这些木棍。如果你们团结在一起，敌人就永远不能将你们打倒；可如果你们互相争斗，便会被敌人轻松战胜。"

团结就是力量。

想一想

◎ 你知道有哪些动物团结在一起就威力无穷吗?

The Farmer and the Quarrelling[①] Sons

A farmer had several sons who were always quarrelling with one another. Try as he might, he could not persuade them to live together in harmony[②]. So he determined[③] to convince[④] them of their folly[⑤] by facts. He asked them to fetch[⑥] a bundle of sticks, and ordered them to break it. All tried and all failed. And then he untied[⑦] the bundle, gave one stick to each of them, and asked them to break it. All of them had no difficulty at all in breaking them.

He then addressed[⑧] to them," My boys, united, you will be more than a match for your enemies. But if you keep quarrelling, you will be easily broken by your enemies."

Unity is strength.

---

① **quarrel**: /ˈkwɒrl/ *v.* 争吵；吵架

② **harmony**: /ˈhɑːməni/ *n.* 和睦；和谐

③ **determine**: /dɪˈtɜːmɪn/ *v.* 决定；确定

④ **convince**: /kənˈvɪns/ *v.* 使确信；使相信

⑤ **folly**: /ˈfɒli/ *n.* 愚蠢；愚蠢的想法（或事情、行为）

⑥ **fetch**: /fetʃ/ *v.* （去）拿来；（去）请来

⑦ **untie**: /ʌnˈtaɪ/ *v.* 打开；解开

⑧ **address**: /əˈdres/ *v.* 对……讲话

38. 老婆子与医生

得了眼病的**老婆子**请**医生**来为自己看病。那医生每次来老婆子家为她涂药时，总趁着老婆子闭着眼顺便偷走一些家具。等到老婆子的眼病好了，医生便向她索要医药费。老婆子不肯付，于是就被医生带到了法官那里。老婆子对法官说：“医生并没有把我的病治好，因为以前我还能看见家里的物品，可现在却一件也看不到了。”

贪得无厌的人总是会不知不觉地留下罪证。

The Old Woman and the Doctor

An old woman asked a doctor to treat her eye illness. Every time the doctor came to visit her, he would steal a piece of furniture[①] out of the house as the old woman closed her eyes. When the old woman's eyes were cured, the doctor asked her to pay the bill. But the old woman refused, so the doctor took her to the magistrate[②]. The old woman explained to the magistrate, "The doctor did not cure me, because I was able to see valuable things in my house before, but I am not able to see a single thing in it now."

The greedy[③] will always unconsciously leave evidence[④] of their crimes[⑤].

---

① **furniture**: /ˈfɜːnɪtʃə/ *n.* （可移动的）家具

② **magistrate**: /ˈmædʒɪstreɪt/ *n.* 地方执法官

③ **greedy**: /ˈɡriːdi/ *adj.* 贪婪的；贪心的

④ **evidence**: /ˈevɪdəns/ *n.* 证明；证据

⑤ **crime**: /kraɪm/ *n.* 犯罪活动；罪行

39. 老妇人与她的女佣

有个节俭的**老妇人**雇了几个**女佣**来帮忙。每天清晨，家里的公鸡一叫，老妇人就会叫女佣们起床干活。女佣们没日没夜地工作，累得筋疲力尽，便痛恨起那只公鸡。一天夜里，女佣们一起把那只公鸡杀了。可公鸡死后，老妇人不知道鸡鸣的时间，总在深夜叫女佣们起来干活，女佣们变得更加忙碌了。

许多人的不幸往往是自己造成的。

知识岛：古代人的计时方法

◎ 在古代，人们除了用公鸡报时，还发明了不少有趣的东西来播报时间。像是用水滴或沙子计算时间的漏壶，还有燃烧特制的盘香测量时长的香钟。

The Old Woman and Her Maids[1]

A thrifty[2] old woman hired[3] several maids to work for her. Every morning, the woman woke them up and asked them to work as soon as the cock crowed[4]. They worked day and night and felt exhausted[5], so they started to hate the cock. One night, the maids caught the cock and killed it. But after that, things got even worse. Not knowing the time without cock crowing, the mistress woke them up earlier than ever and set them to work in the middle of the night. The maids became even busier than before.

Some acts are often self-defeating[6].

---

① **maid**: /meɪd/ *n.*（家中的）女佣，女仆，侍女

② **thrifty**: /ˈθrɪfti/ *adj.* 节约的，节俭的

③ **hire**: /ˈhaɪə/ *v.* 租用；雇用

④ **crow**: /krəʊ/ *v.*（公鸡）鸣叫，打鸣

⑤ **exhaust**: /ɪɡˈzɔːst/ *v.* 使筋疲力尽；使疲惫不堪

⑥ **self-defeating**: /ˌselfdɪˈfiːtɪŋ/ *adj.* 适得其反的；弄巧成拙的

40. 女人与母鸡

有个**女人**养了一只**母鸡**，这只母鸡每天都生一个蛋。女人常常琢磨如何能每天得到两个鸡蛋。最后她决定每天多喂母鸡一倍的大麦。结果，母鸡从那天开始变得越来越肥，一个鸡蛋也生不出来了。

贪欲不仅不会让我们得到更多，反而还会失去已经拥有的。

The Woman and the Hen

A woman possessed a hen that gave her an egg every day. She often pondered [1] how she might obtain [2] two eggs daily instead of one. At last, she decided to give the hen a double allowance [3] of barley [4]. From that day on, the hen became fatter and fatter, and never laid another egg.

Greed cannot bring us more but take what we already have.

① **ponder**: /ˈpɒndə/ *v.* 沉思；琢磨

② **obtain**: /əbˈteɪn/ *v.*（尤指经努力）获得

③ **allowance**: /əˈlaʊns/ *n.* 补贴；补助

④ **barley**: /ˈbɑːli/ *n.* 大麦；大麦粒

41. 猪与羊群

有一只**猪**溜进了一个**羊群**，每天和羊群一起吃饭睡觉。一天，牧人来抓猪，猪一边挣扎，一边哀号。一只羊责备他说："牧人经常来捉我们，也会像这样拽我们，可我们从来不会像你那样吵闹。"猪却回答："我和你们的情况可完全不同啊。他捉你们是要你们的毛，捉我是要我的肉哇。"

真正的危险不是关系到钱财，而是攸关性命。

The Pig and the Sheep

A pig found his way into a flock[1] of sheep, and lived with them, sleeping and eating under the same roof. One day, the shepherd came to catch him. The pig struggled and squealed[2]. A sheep rebuked[3] him for making such a noise, and said to him, "The shepherd catches us regularly[4] and drags us off like that, and we don't make any fuss." The pig replied, " But my case and yours are altogether[5] different. He only wants you for wool[6], but he wants me for bacon[7]."

The real danger has nothing to do with wealth, but life.

---

① **flock**: /flɒk/ *n.*（羊或鸟）群；（尤指同类人的）一大群

② **squeal**: /skwiːl/ *v.* 发出长而尖的声音；尖叫

③ **rebuke**: /rɪˈbjuːk/ *v.* 指责；批评

④ **regularly**: /ˈreɡjələli/ *adv.* 有规律地；经常

⑤ **altogether**: /ˌɔːltəˈɡeðə/ *adv.*（用以强调）完全

⑥ **wool**: /wʊl/ *n.*（羊等的）绒，毛

⑦ **bacon**: /ˈbeɪkən/ *n.* 咸猪肉；熏猪肉

42. 鹿与他的倒影

一只口渴的**鹿**在池塘边喝水，水里映照出他的**倒影**。他先是为自己修长又美丽的鹿角得意扬扬，之后又为自己短小纤细的腿而闷闷不乐。这时一只狮子蹿了出来。鹿撒腿就跑。在空旷的原野上，鹿一下子就把狮子甩在了身后。可到了树林，鹿角被树枝缠住，狮子终于抓到了鹿。

在临死之前鹿哀叹道：“我太不幸了。原先被我看不起的腿救了我，可我引以为傲的角却害了我。”

尺有所短，寸有所长。

The Stag[1] and His Reflection[2]

A thirsty stag went down to a pool to drink. As he bent[3] over the surface, he saw his own reflection in the water, and was struck with the admiration[4] for his fine spreading[5] antlers[6]. While at the same time, he felt sad for the weakness and slenderness[7] of his legs. At this moment, a lion showed up. The stag started to run. He soon ran away from the lion in the open field. But when coming into woods, he was caught by his antlers in the branches. The lion seized him at last.

The stag cried with his last breath, " How unfortunate I am! The legs which I despised[8] might have saved my life, while the antlers which I was proud of brought me death."

Everyone has his strengths and weakness.

---

① **stag**: /stæg/ *n.* 成年雄鹿

② **reflection**: /rɪˈflekʃn/ *n.* 映像；映照出的影像

③ **bend**: /bend/ *v.* （使）倾斜，偏向；弯曲

④ **admiration**: /ˌædməˈreɪʃn/ *n.* 钦佩；赞赏

⑤ **spread**: /spred/ *v.* 展开；打开

⑥ **antler**: /ˈæntlə/ *n.* 鹿角

⑦ **slenderness**: /ˈslendənəs/ *n.* 纤细；细长

⑧ **despise**: /dɪˈspaɪz/ *v.* 鄙视；蔑视

43. 鹿与洞里的狮子

一只**鹿**为了逃过猎人的追捕，跑进了一个山洞。不幸的是，那山洞里住着一只**狮子**，鹿刚一进去就被狮子捉住了。临死之前，鹿高喊着：“我真是倒霉透了，以为躲过了猎人，却将自己送进了狮子的口中。”

有些人为了逃避小的危险，却将自己置于更大的危险之中。

想一想

◎ 遇到麻烦的事情，我们除了逃跑，还能做些什么？

The Deer and the Lion in the Cave

In order to escape from the hunter, a deer took refuge[1] in a cave. Unfortunately there lived a lion. The lion seized him soon after he came in. Before the deer died he cried, "How unlucky I am! I escaped from the hunter, but I put myself into a lion's mouth."

Some people may expose[2] themselves to greater dangers in order to escape small ones.

① **refuge**: /ˈrefjuːdʒ/ *n.* 庇护；避难所

② **expose**: /ɪkˈspəʊz/ *v.* 暴露；使曝光

44. 小山羊与狼

一只掉队的**小山羊**被**狼**捉住了。小山羊便对狼说："反正我已经是你手里的猎物了，可不可以让我享受最后的一点快乐？你来吹箫，我来跳最后一支舞。"于是狼拿出箫吹了起来，小山羊跳起了舞。守护羊群的猎狗听到箫声跑来把狼赶跑了。狼一边逃跑，一边说道："我真活该！本是一个屠夫，却偏要干吹箫的事。"

不分辨时机做事的人，最终会失去自己拥有的东西。

The Kid[1] and the Wolf

A little kid strayed[2] from the flock and was caught by a wolf. The kid said to the wolf, " I know that I can't escape from you. Could you let me enjoy the last happiness before death? Please pipe[3] me a tune to my last dance before I die." So the wolf took out his pipe and began to play, while the kid danced. Some hounds[4] who guarded[5] the flock heard the sound. They came up and drove the wolf away. The wolf ran away saying, " It's what I thoroughly deserved. I'm a butcher, but I tried to be a piper."

People who failed to do the right things at the right time will eventually[6] lose what they have.

---

① **kid**: /kɪd/ *n.* 小孩；小山羊，小羚羊

② **stray**: /streɪ/ *v.* 迷路；偏离

③ **pipe**: /paɪp/ *n.* 管子；笛（子）；管乐器

v. 用管乐器演奏；尖声说；尖声唱

④ **hound**: /haʊnd/ *n.* 猎犬，猎狗

⑤ **guard**: /gɑːd/ *v.* 守卫；保卫

⑥ **eventually**: /ɪˈventʃuəli/ *adv.* 最后，终于

45. 两个仇人

从前，有**两个仇人**坐了同一艘船。他们一人坐在船头，一人坐在船尾。突然海上风雨交加，船摇摇摆摆地快要沉了。这时，船尾的人问船夫，船的哪一头会先沉。船夫回答，船头会先遭殃。船尾的人便高喊："能在死之前看到我的仇人先死，那我也死而无憾了。"

有些人将复仇看得比生命都重要。

知识岛：复仇的故事

◎ 著名的大作家莎士比亚也写了一个关于复仇的故事叫《哈姆雷特》。在那个故事里，王子遇见了死去父亲的灵魂，并知道了父亲被杀害的秘密。于是，王子开始了一段曲折又悲惨的复仇之路。

The Two Enemies

Two men, deadly enemies to each other, were sailing in the same boat, one sitting at the prow① and the other at the stern②. Suddenly it was raining and blowing hard. The boat swayed③ and was about to sink. At this time, the man at the stern asked the boatman which part of the boat would sink first. The boatman replied that the prow would suffer first. Hearing this, the man at the stern shouted, " Death would not be grievous④ to me, if I could only see my enemy die before me."

Some people regard revenge⑤ more important than life.

---

① **prow**: /praʊ/ *n.* 船头

② **stern**: /stɜːn/ *n.* 船尾

③ **sway**: /sweɪ/ *v.* （使）摇摆，摇动

④ **grievous**: /ˈgriːvəs/ *adj.* 令人悲伤的，使人痛苦的

⑤ **revenge**: /rɪˈvendʒ/ *n.* 报复；报仇

46. 蝰蛇与水蛇

蝰蛇常常到河边喝水。住在河里的**水蛇**非常不高兴，认为蝰蛇霸占了自己的领地。他们便因此吵了起来，并约定打一架，胜者即拥有那条河以及岸边的领地。那些讨厌水蛇的青蛙知道这件事后，跑来鼓励蝰蛇，还答应为他助战。

战斗开始了，蝰蛇与水蛇打了起来，可青蛙们却站在一旁，除了叫唤什么也不干。蝰蛇胜利后，便责怪青蛙。可青蛙们却说："我们虽然没有用行动帮助你，但我们用了声音呀。"

真正的帮助要有真正的行动。

The Viper[1] and the Water-Snake

There was a viper who used to go to a river to drink. The water-snake who lived in the river was furious[2] that the viper encroached[3] on his territory[4]. They quarrelled and finally decided to fight it out, agreeing that both the water and its banks would be awarded[5] to the winner. Some frogs, who hated the water-snake, learned of this.They came to the viper and promised to offer him their aids.

But when the battle[6] finally began and the viper grappled[7] with the water-snake, the frogs did nothing except croaking[8]. In the end, the viper won, but he was furious with the frogs. The frogs then said to him, " We haven't used our actions to help you, but we have used our voice."

Real help requires real action.

① **viper**: /ˈvaɪpə/ *n.* 蝰蛇（一种小毒蛇）

② **furious**: /ˈfjʊəriəs/ *adj.* 狂怒的；暴怒的

③ **encroach**: /ɪnˈkrəʊtʃ/ *v.* 侵占（某人的时间）；侵犯（某人的权利）

④ **territory**: /ˈterətri/ *n.* 领土；领地

⑤ **award**: /əˈwɔːd/ *v.* 授予；奖励

⑥ **battle**: /ˈbætl/ *n.* 战役；战斗

⑦ **grapple**: /ˈgræpl/ *v.* 扭打；搏斗

⑧ **croak**: /krəʊk/ *v.* 发出（像青蛙的）低沉沙哑声；呱呱地叫

47. 医生与病人

一个**医生**给**病人**治病，可病人还是死了。他对那些送葬的人说道："这人如果戒了酒，治疗一下肠胃，就不会死了。"

在场的一个人回答："先生，这些话你应该在病人还活着的时候说。"

当别人遇到困难时，应及时给予帮助，而不该在事后去说闲话。

The Doctor and the Patient[①]

Once a doctor tried to cure a patient, but failed. After the patient died, the doctor said to the patient's relatives[②] on the funeral[③], "The man would not have died if he had given up drinking wine and had his stomach treated."

Someone in the crowd[④] then said to the doctor, " Sir, you should have given him the advice while he is still alive."

We should offer our help when there is need of it, instead of gossiping afterwards.

---

① **patient**: /ˈpeɪʃnt/ *n.* 病人

② **relative**: /ˈrelətɪv/ *n.* 亲戚；亲属

③ **funeral**: /ˈfjuːnərl/ *n.* 葬礼；丧礼

④ **crowd**: /kraʊd/ *n.* 人群；一伙人

48. 学马叫的鹞子

鹞子原本有一种美妙的叫声，但他听见**马**的嘶叫后，觉得非常好听，便开始学马那样嘶叫。可最后，鹞子不但没有学会马叫，连自己原本的叫声都忘记了。

好高骛远的人会失去自己原本拥有的东西。

知识岛：动物的叫声

◎ 世界上有很多动物确实拥有奇特的叫声，像是某种鱼能发出婴孩的啼哭声，某种蛇能发出拨浪鼓的摇晃声。

The Kite[1] Who Learned to Neigh[2]

The kite once had a wonderful voice. But one day he heard a horse neighing beautifully, so he tried to imitate[3] it. Try as he might, he simply couldn't attain[4] the same voice as the horse, and at the same time he lost his own.

An over-ambitious[5] person will lose what he originally[6] had.

---

① **kite**: /kaɪt/ *n.* 鸢（中国古代又将鸢称作鹞子）

② **neigh**: /neɪ/ *v.*（马）嘶鸣

③ **imitate**: /ˈɪmɪteɪt/ *v.* 模仿

④ **attain**: /əˈteɪn/ *v.*（通常经过努力）获得，得到

⑤ **ambitious**: /æmˈbɪʃəs/ *adj.* 志向远大的；雄心勃勃的

⑥ **originally**: /əˈrɪdʒənəli/ *adv.* 原本；起初

49. 捕鸟人与毒蛇

一天，**捕鸟人**拿着网子去捕鸟。他在一棵高高的树上发现了一只漂亮的鸟。于是，他盯着那只鸟，举起套着网的杆子，一步步向鸟靠近。可一不小心，捕鸟人踩到了一条**毒蛇**，被毒蛇狠狠咬了一口。临死之前，捕鸟人喃喃自语道：“我真倒霉，光想着捕鸟，却丢了自己的性命。”

害人也会让自己陷入不幸。

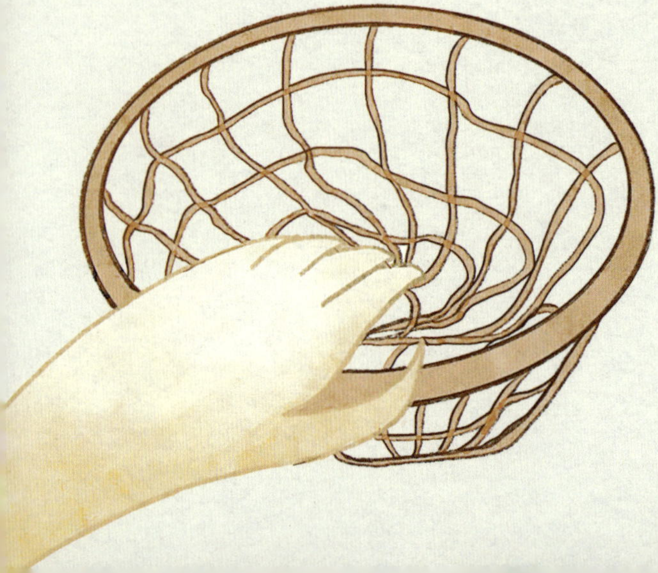

The Bird Catcher and the Viper

One day, a bird catcher, taking his net, went out to catch birds. Then he saw a beautiful bird up high in a tree. He stared up at it, held up the net, and moved to it step by step. But by accident, he stepped on a viper who gave him an angry bite. Before he breathed his last, the bird catcher said, " Unlucky me. I was focusing[1] on stalking[2] the bird, but lost my own life."

While hurting others, one might hurt himself.

① **focus**: /ˈfɒkəs/ *v.* 专注

② **stalk**: /stɔːk/ *v.* 偷偷接近，潜近（猎物或人）

50. 马与驴子

从前，有一个人赶着一匹**马**和一头**驴子**去送货。赶路途中，驴子对马说：“请帮我分担一些重物吧，我快累死了。”马却摇摇头，看着驴子精疲力竭地倒下，死掉了。之后，主人把全部货物和从死掉的驴子身上扒下的皮，都放在了马的背上。

这时，马悲伤地说：“我真不幸啊！因为不愿帮驴子负担一些重量，现在就要背上所有的货物。”

强者需要和弱者合作，才能更好地生存。

The Horse and the Donkey

Once upon a time, a man drove a horse and a donkey to deliver ① goods. On the way, the donkey said to the horse, " Please help me with some of the heavy loads. They are killing me." The horse shook his head and watched the donkey fall exhausted ② and died. After that, the owner put all the goods and the skin from the dead donkey on the horse's back.

At that moment, the horse said sadly, " How unfortunate! I have to carry all the goods because I don't want to help the donkey share some weight."

The strong also need to cooperate ③ with the weak in order to better survive ④.

---

① **deliver**: /dɪˈlɪvə/ *v.* 运送；递送

② **exhausted**: /ɪɡˈzɔːstɪd/ *adj.* 筋疲力尽的；疲惫不堪的

③ **cooperate**: /kəʊˈɒpəreɪt/ *v.* 合作；协作

④ **survive**: /səˈvaɪv/ *v.* 生存；幸存

51. 士兵与马

打仗的时候，一个**士兵**用大麦细心地喂养他的**马**。等战争一结束，那马便被拉去做苦工，搬运很重的货物。后来军号吹响了，又要打仗了，士兵给马套上马鞍，全副武装准备去战斗。这时，马却没有了力气，摔倒在地。他对士兵说道："你还是赶紧去找一匹战马吧，因为你之前已经把我当成一头驴子了，还怎能指望把我变回一匹战马呢？"

要学会居安思危。

想一想

◎ 为什么被当作驴子的马不能再做战马了？

The Soldier[①] and His Horse

During the war, a soldier fed his horse carefully with barley. When the war came to an end, the horse was sent to carry heavy cargo. Some time later, the trumpet[②] summoned[③] and war came again. The soldier put the bridle[④] and saddle[⑤] back on his steed[⑥], sharpened his sword[⑦] and got ready for the war. But when he was about to mount[⑧] it, the horse collapsed and fell to his knees, no longer equal to the burden. The horse said to his owner, " Go and find a new steed, for you have transformed me from a horse into a donkey. Do you really think you can change me back again?"

We must be prepared for danger in times of peace.

---

① **soldier**: /ˈsəʊldʒə/ *n.* 军人；士兵

② **trumpet**: /ˈtrʌmpɪt/ *n.* 小号；喇叭

③ **summon**: /ˈsʌmən/ *v.* 传唤；召唤

④ **bridle**: /ˈbraɪdl/ *n.* 马勒；马笼头

⑤ **saddle**: /ˈsædl/ *n.* 马鞍；车座

⑥ **steed**: /stiːd/ *n.* 坐骑

⑦ **sword**: /sɔːd/ *n.* 剑；刀

⑧ **mount**: /maʊnt/ *v.* 登上；骑上

52. 芦苇与橄榄树

有一天，**芦苇**和**橄榄树**争论谁更强大。橄榄树嘲笑芦苇软弱无能，一遇到风就点头哈腰。芦苇不说话。这时，一阵狂风吹来。芦苇随风摆动，逃过一劫。而橄榄树则迎风不动，结果被风连根拔起，倒了下来。

遇到风险时，退让也许比硬斗更安全。

The Reed and the Olive[1] Tree

One day, a reed got into an argument with an olive tree about who was stronger. The olive tree laughed at the reed for his being weak, since he was naturally inclined[2] to yield[3] to every breeze[4]. The reed did not respond. At this moment, the wind began to blow fiercely[5]. The reed bent with the wind and left unharmed, while the olive tree which stayed still was torn[6] up by her roots and toppled[7] over.

When encountering[8] risks, giving in may be safer than confronting the tough with toughness.

---

① **olive**: /ˈɒlɪv/ *n.* 橄榄；橄榄树

② **incline**: /ɪnˈklaɪn/ *v.* （使）倾向于，有……的趋势

③ **yield**: /jiːld/ *v.* 屈服；让步

④ **breeze**: /briːz/ *n.* 微风；和风

⑤ **fiercely**: /ˈfɪəsli/ *adv.* 凶猛地；猛烈地

⑥ **tear**: /teə/ *v.* 撕裂；撕碎

⑦ **topple**: /ˈtɒpl/ *v.* 倒塌，倒下

⑧ **encounter**: /ɪnˈkaʊntə/ *v.* 遭遇，遇到

53. 两只屎壳郎

一个小岛上生活着两只吃牛粪的**屎壳郎**。冬天来了，一只屎壳郎对另一只说，他想飞到大陆去过冬，这样小岛上的屎壳郎就可以有充足的牛粪过冬了，如果他找到丰富的食物，将会带些回来。

他飞到大陆，发现了许多新鲜的牛粪，于是在那里美滋滋地度过了冬天。等他又飞回到小岛时，已经变得又肥又壮。小岛上的屎壳郎便谴责他不守信用，什么都没有带回来。他却回答：“你可不能责怪我，而是要责怪那地方的风气，因为在那里只可以吃东西，不能往外带东西。”

那些不信守承诺的朋友是不可信赖的。

The Two Dung Beetles[1]

There were two dung beetles on a small island, fed on bull's manure[2]. Winter was approaching, so one of the dung beetles said to the other, he wanted to go to the mainland, so that the one stayed on the island could have enough manure for the winter. If he happened to find plenty of food over there, he would bring some back.

The dung beetle then moved to the mainland and found a lot of manure that was all moist[3] and fresh. He settled down and had plenty[4] to eat. When winter passed, he flew back to the small island. When the dung beetle on it found him strong and fat, he asked him why he had not kept his promise. The other dung beetle replied, "Don't blame me! There is a custom that you can eat there, but you are not allowed to take any food away."

Friends who do not keep their promises are untrustworthy[5].

---

① **dung beetle**: /dʌŋˈbiːtl/ *n.* 蜣螂，俗称屎壳郎，又名粪金龟

② **manure**: /məˈnjʊə/ *n.* 粪肥；肥料

③ **moist**: /mɔɪst/ *adj.* 微湿的；湿润的

④ **plenty**: /ˈplenti/ *n.* 大量；丰富；充足

⑤ **untrustworthy**: /ʌnˈtrʌstˌwɜːði/ *adj.* 不可靠的；不能信赖（或信任）的

54. 螃蟹与狐狸

一只**螃蟹**离开了大海，想要在海边生活。这时，一只饥饿的**狐狸**马上捉住了螃蟹。螃蟹在死前哀叹："我真是活该！我本来应该生活在大海里，却偏要上岸。"

认清自己，量力而行。

知识岛：螃蟹的居住地

◎ 螃蟹除了生活在大海里，其实还有一些能生活在溪流的石头下或是潮湿的泥洞里。

The Crab① and the Fox

A crab once left the sea and wanted to live on the shore. A hungry fox immediately grabbed him. As he was about to be eaten, the crab exclaimed②, " This is just what I deserve! I am a creature of the sea, but try to live on land."

Know yourself and act with prudence③.

① **crab**: /kræb/ *n.* 蟹，螃蟹

② **exclaim**: /ɪkˈskleɪm/ *v.*（由于强烈的情感或痛苦而）惊叫，呼喊

③ **prudence**: /ˈpruːdns/ *n.* 谨慎

55. 核桃树

有棵结满果实的**核桃树**长在路旁。路过的人们都用石头砸他，以获得树上的核桃。核桃树叹息道："我真是倒霉。每年人们开心地享用我的果实，可他们却用如此恶劣的方式来对待我。"

要善待那些对你好的人。

The Walnut[1] Tree

A walnut tree standing by the roadside bore an abundant crop of fruit. People passing by used to knock them off by throwing stones at the tree. The walnut tree piteously[2] exclaimed, "Woe[3] is me! People gladly enjoy my fruit every year, but they have such a terrible way of showing their gratitude."

Be kind to those who do good to you.

---

① **walnut**: /ˈwɔːlnʌt/ *n.* 核桃；核桃树

② **piteously**: /ˈpɪtiəsli/ *adv.* 可怜巴巴地

③ **woe**: /wəʊ/ *n.* 悲伤；悲哀

56. 小偷与公鸡

几个**小偷**溜进一户人家，却什么值钱的东西也没找到，除了一只**公鸡**。他们便把公鸡抓走了。当小偷们要杀公鸡时，公鸡恳求小偷们说：“我对人们是有好处的，天亮的时候，我可以把人们叫醒去工作。”小偷们回答：“单凭这一点，你就非死不可了。因为那些被你叫醒的人妨碍了我们偷东西。”

那些对好人有益的事往往对坏人有害。

The Thieves and the Rooster[①]

Some thieves broke into a house, and found nothing but a rooster. They took him away. Later, when they were prepared to kill him, the rooster begged the thieves to let him go, claiming, " I'm useful to people. I can wake them up to work at dawn[②]." The thieves replied, " All the more reason to kill you. When you wake them up, you prevent[③] us from robbing their houses."

Things beneficial[④] to honest folk may frustrate[⑤] wicked people .

---

① **rooster**: /ˈruːstə/ *n.* 雄鸡；公鸡

② **dawn**: /dɔːn/ *n.* 黎明；拂晓

③ **prevent**: /prɪˈvent/ *v.* 阻止；阻碍；阻挠

④ **beneficial**: /ˌbenɪˈfɪʃl/ *adj.* 有利的；有益的

⑤ **frustrate**: /frʌˈstreɪt/ *v.* 使灰心，使气馁；挫败

57. 寒鸦与狐狸

有只饥饿的**寒鸦**落在一棵无花果树上。他发现无花果还是青的，便在那里等候果子成熟。

狐狸看见寒鸦坐了很久，得知缘由后，狐狸说道："喂，朋友，你可真是糊涂，光靠着希望可填不饱肚子。"

盲目地等待却不去努力只会一无所获。

想一想

◎ 希望既然不能填饱我们的肚子，那么希望能带给我们什么呢？

The Jackdaw[1] and the Fox

A hungry jackdaw alighted[2] on a fig[3] tree. He discovered[4] that the figs were not ripe[5] yet, so he waited in the hope that the figs would ripen.

A fox saw the jackdaw sitting there. Learning the reason of his doing so, he said to him, " Hey, my friend, it is a big mistake you are making. Hope may lead you on[6] at first but then leave you empty-handed."

Waiting blindly without working hard you will get nothing.

---

① **jackdaw**: /ˈdʒækdɔː/ *n.* 寒鸦

② **alight**: /əˈlaɪt/ *v.* 降落；飞落

③ **fig**: /fɪɡ/ *n.* 无花果

④ **discover**: /dɪˈskʌvə/ *v.* 发现；发觉

⑤ **ripe**: /raɪp/ *adj.* 成熟的

⑥ **lead sb. on**: 误导某人；蒙骗某人

58. 寒鸦与借来的羽毛

宙斯准备选一个最美的鸟王。评选的日子来临前，所有的鸟都来到一条河边梳洗打扮。

一只**寒鸦**觉得自己十分难看，便去捡其他鸟掉下的**羽毛**，插在自己身上。于是寒鸦便成了鸟群中最美丽的鸟。宙斯就将寒鸦封为鸟王。

这个消息让其他鸟十分生气。他们于是把自己的羽毛从寒鸦的身上拔走，寒鸦又变回了原来的模样。

依靠别人得到的风光是假象，失去依靠后就会原形毕露。

The Jackdaw and the Borrowed Feathers

Zeus was going to choose the most beautiful bird as the king. Before the election[①] day, all the birds came to the river, freshened themselves up and put decorations on for the great occasion.

A jackdaw, who felt he was very ugly, picked up the feathers[②] dropped by other birds and stuck them on his own body. With all the feathers, the jackdaw changed into the most beautiful one in the flock. So Zeus named him the king of the birds.

This decision made all the other birds very angry. So they each plucked[③] from him their own feathers. Then the jackdaw changed back to his original appearance.

Fake beauty is doomed to fade fast.

① **election**: /ɪˈlekʃn/ *n.* 选举

② **feather**: /ˈfeðə/ *n.* 羽毛；翎毛

③ **pluck**: /plʌk/ *v.* 拔

59. 寒鸦与鸽子

寒鸦看见**鸽子**在窝里好吃好喝的，便将自己染白，潜入鸽子窝，同鸽子们一起生活。在鸽子窝里，他不曾发出过声音，鸽子们也就从来没有怀疑过寒鸦的身份。可有一回，他不小心叫了一声，鸽子们立刻认出了寒鸦，将他赶出了鸽子窝。寒鸦找不到东西吃，只好又回到原先的寒鸦群中。但寒鸦们认不出染成白色的他，也把他赶走了。

贪婪会让我们一无所有。

The Jackdaw and the Doves[1]

A jackdaw found that the doves in a dovecote[2] were abundantly provided with food, so he dyed[3] himself white and joined them in order to share their food. So long as the jackdaw kept quiet in the dovecote, the doves thought he was another dove and accepted him. But one day, he forgot to keep quiet and let out a squawk[4]. The doves then recognized[5] who he was and they pecked[6] at him until he went away. Unable to find food, he had to go back to the jackdaws. But because they could not recognize him in white, they drove him away.

Greed will deprive[7] us of all the things we have.

---

① **dove**: /dʌv/ *n.* 鸽子

② **dovecote**: /ˈdʌvkɒt/ *n.* 鸽房；鸽舍

③ **dye**: /daɪ/ *v.* 给……染色；染

④ **squawk**: /skwɔːk/ *n.*（尤指鸟受惊时发出的）粗粝的叫声

⑤ **recognize**: /ˈrekəgnaɪz/ *v.* 认出；辨别出

⑥ **peck**: /pek/ *v.* 啄

⑦ **deprive**: /dɪˈpraɪv/ *v.* 剥夺；使丧失

60. 逃走的寒鸦

有人抓住了一只**寒鸦**，把他的脚用绳子绑住送给小孩玩。

寒鸦非常不愿意，趁人们不注意逃回林中。不料脚上的绳子缠住了树枝，他再也飞不起来了。

临死之前，寒鸦哀叹道：“我真是倒霉，不愿成为人的奴隶，却因此丢了性命。”

我们有时以为逃过了危险，可真正的危险却在后头等着我们。

想一想

◎ 如果你是寒鸦，你会选择逃跑还是留在人们的手中？

The Escaped Jackdaw

A man caught a jackdaw and tied his foot with a piece of string①, and then gave him to his children as a pet②.

The jackdaw, however, was very unwilling③ to live with human. So when they let him loose for just a moment, he flew back to his old haunts④. However, the string soon got entangled⑤ in the branches, and the jackdaw was unable to fly any more.

Knowing that it was all up with him, the bird sighed: " How unfortunate! I could not stand being a slave⑥ of human, but lost my life."

We sometimes think we have escaped danger, but actually the real dangers wait ahead of us.

---

① **string**: /strɪŋ/ *n.* 细绳；线

② **pet**: /pet/ *n.* 宠物

③ **unwilling**: /ʌnˈwɪlɪŋ/ *adj.* 不情愿；不愿意

④ **haunt**: /hɔːnt/ *n.* 常去的地方

⑤ **entangle**: /ɪnˈtæŋgl/ *v.* 使纠缠；缠住

⑥ **slave**: /sleɪv/ *n.* 奴隶

61. 渡鸦与蛇

有只饥饿的**渡鸦**正到处找东西吃，这时他看到一条在阳光下睡觉的**蛇**。他便猛扑过去，一把抓住了蛇。不料蛇回头咬了渡鸦一口。渡鸦临死前说道：“我真是傻啊！为了意外得来的食物而丢掉了宝贵的性命。”

有些东西不值得我们用生命去冒险。

The Raven[1] and the Snake

A hungry raven, looking for food, found a snake asleep in the sun. The raven jumped on the snake and grabbed it. But the snake twisted[2] her head and bit him. As he was dying, the raven said, "What a fool I was! The windfall[3] I found has turned out to be fatal."

Do not risk your life for unworthy things.

---

① **raven**: /ˈreɪvn/ *n.* 渡鸦（一种全身黑色的鸦属鸟类）

② **twist**: /twɪst/ *v.* 扭转，转动

③ **windfall**: /ˈwɪndfɔːl/ *n.* 意外之财；意外获得的东西

62. 生病的渡鸦

渡鸦生了重病，便对母亲说道："不要悲伤，母亲，请你快去求众神帮忙吧。"母亲却回答："儿呀，众神里哪家的肉你没偷过，哪个神又会可怜你呢？"

如果平时总在树立敌人，一旦陷入危险，就没有朋友会来帮忙。

The Sick Raven

A raven was seriously ill. He said to his mother, " Don't be sad mum, please hurry up and ask the gods for help." But his mother replied, " My son, you have stolen the meat from all the gods. Who of them will sympathise[①] with you?"

If we are always making enemies, once we are in danger, no one will come to help.

① **sympathise**: /ˈsɪmpəθaɪz/ *v.* 同情；怜悯

63. 落网的云雀

一只**云雀**落入网中，她哀叹道：“我真是不幸的鸟呀！我没偷人家的金子，也没偷人家的银子，更没偷人家宝贝的东西，只是偷了一粒小小的谷子，却让自己丢了性命。”

贪小便宜吃大亏。

想一想

◎ 云雀除了贪小便宜，她还做错了什么？

The Lark[1] in a Net

A lark fell into a trap, and she lamented[2], " I'm such an unlucky bird! I didn't steal other people's gold or silver, nor did I steal their treasures. I just stole a small grain[3], which brings death to me."

Penny[4] wise and pound[5] foolish.

---

① **lark**: /lɑːk/ *n.* 云雀，百灵鸟

② **lament**: /ləˈment/ *v.* 痛惜；悲叹

③ **grain**: /ɡreɪn/ *n.* 谷物；谷粒

④ **penny**: /ˈpeni/ *n.* （英国）便士（最小的货币单位）

⑤ **pound**: /paʊnd/ *n.* 镑（英国等国家的货币单位）

64. 农夫的孩子与田螺

农夫的孩子烤**田螺**吃。当他听见田螺在火中吱吱地响时便说道："啊，可怜的东西，你们的家都被烧了，还有心情唱歌。"

不分场合的行为有时会受到指责。

The Farmer's Boy and the Snails①

A farmer's boy was roasting② snails. While hearing them sizzling③ in the fire, he said, " You poor things, how could you find the heart to sing when your houses are burning?"

Untimely④ behaviours may be ridiculed⑤.

---

① **snail**: /sneɪl/ *n.* 蜗牛；螺

② **roast**: /rəʊst/ *v.* 烘；烤

③ **sizzle**: /ˈsɪzl/ *v.* 发出（油煎食物的）嗞嗞声

④ **untimely**: /ʌnˈtaɪmli/ *adj.* 不合时宜的

⑤ **ridicule**: /ˈrɪdɪkjuːl/ *v.* 嘲笑；奚落；讥笑

65. 两只狗

猎人养了**两只狗**，一只用来打猎，一只用来看门。猎人每次带猎狗出门时，只要抓到点什么，都会分给看门狗。猎狗对此非常不满，便责怪看门狗说：“为什么我要到处奔波，而你却什么也不做就能得到食物？”看门狗说道：“为什么你要责怪我呢？是主人让我不要去打猎，也是他给我那些猎物的呀。”

不要指责小孩的懒惰，因为那可能是他的父母将他养成那样的。

The Two Dogs

The hunter has two dogs, one for hunting and the other as the doorkeeper. Every time the hunter took the hunting dog out and came back with something, he would share with the watch dog. The hunting dog was so dissatisfied① that he blamed the watch dog, " Why should I run all over the place trying to find food, but you can get it without doing anything?" The watch dog replied, "Why do you blame me? It is the master who does not take me to hunt but gives me the food instead."

Don´t blame a child for his laziness②, because his parents may have brought him up in that way.

---

① **dissatisfied**: /dɪsˈsætɪsfaɪd/ *adj.* （对……）不满的；不高兴的

② **laziness**: /ˈleɪzinəs/ *n.* 怠惰，懒散

66. 狗、公鸡与狐狸

公鸡和一只**狗**成了好朋友，他们相约一起赶路。到了晚上，公鸡跳到树上睡觉，狗就在树下的树洞里过夜。天一亮，公鸡像往常那样啼叫。有只**狐狸**听到了鸡叫，就想吃掉这只鸡。狐狸来到树下，恭敬地对公鸡说："多么优美的声音，我真想拥抱你，和你一起唱歌。你愿意下来吗？"公鸡回答："请你先去问问我那个在树洞里的朋友吧。如果他答应的话，我会立马飞下来。"狐狸就来到树洞前，狗突然跳起来，一把抓住狐狸，将他咬成碎片。

聪明的人总能化解危机。

想一想

◎ 公鸡是如何一步一步化险为夷的？

The Dog, the Rooster and the Fox

A dog and a rooster had become friends and agreed to travel together. When night fell, they took shelter in the woods. The rooster took his seat up in the branches of a tree while the dog went to sleep in a hollow at the foot of the tree. When the morning dawned, the rooster crowed loudly as he usually did. A fox heard the rooster and wanted to make a meal of him. He came up and stood at the foot of the tree and shouted respectfully[①] to the rooster, " What a beautiful voice you have. I really want to hug you and sing with you. Would you come down?" The rooster replied, " Go and ask my friend in the hollow of the tree. If he agrees, I will come down immediately." When the fox came to the hollow, the dog suddenly leaped[②] up, grabbed the fox, and tore him into pieces.

Wise people can always resolve the crisis.

---

① **respectfully**: /rɪˈspektfli/ *adv.* 恭敬地；有礼貌地

② **leap**: /liːp/ *v.* 跳，跳跃

67. 狗与牡蛎

有一只**狗**常常偷吃鸡蛋。一天，他在海边看见一个**牡蛎**，以为那是鸡蛋，便张大了嘴，一口把牡蛎吞了下去。

不久，狗的肚子就疼得厉害，他说："我真是活该，以为一切圆的东西都是鸡蛋。"

鲁莽行事往往不会得到好的结果。

The Dog and the Oyster[①]

There was a dog who used to steal and swallow[②] eggs. One day he came across an oyster on the shore, and supposed it to be an egg. The dog opened his mouth, took a great gulp[③], and swallowed the oyster.

Soon afterwards, suffering great pain in his stomach, the dog remarked, " I really deserve it. That's what I get for thinking that anything round must be an egg."

Those who act in haste[④] often fall into danger.

① **oyster**: /ˈɔɪstə/ *n.* 牡蛎，蚝

② **swallow**: /ˈswɒləʊ/ *v.* 吞下；咽下

③ **gulp**: /ɡʌlp/ *n.* 一大口；吞咽

④ **haste**: /heɪst/ *n.* 匆忙，仓促

68. 狼与睡着的狗

一只狼看见一只狗躺在谷仓前面睡觉。狼想吃了他。狗哀求道：“我现在还很瘦小。如果你肯等到我的主人举办婚礼的那天，我就有许多东西可以吃，会变得白白胖胖的，那时你就可以大吃一顿了。”狼觉得狗说得有道理，便离开了。

不久之后，狼回来了，却看见那只狗睡在了谷仓的上面。狼要狗遵守曾经的约定。那狗说道：“喂，狼呀，假如你以后再看到我睡在谷仓的前面，请你不要再等什么婚礼了。”

聪明的人会防止再犯那些曾让自己陷入麻烦的错误。

The Wolf and the Sleeping Dog

A wolf spot a dog sleeping in front of the barn[1]. When he was ready to devour the dog, the dog begged the wolf to let him go, "Now I am thin and scrawny[2]. My owners are about to celebrate[3] a wedding[4], so if you could wait until then, I'll get fattened up and you can make a good meal of me." The wolf thought that the dog's words were reasonable[5] and went away.

When the wolf came back a few days later, he saw the dog sleeping on the barn. The wolf shouted to the dog, reminding him of their agreement, but the dog simply said, " Wolf, if you ever catch me sleeping in front of the barn again, don't wait for a wedding."

When the intelligent[6] people escape from some threatening[7] situation, they will be on guard in the future.

---

① **barn**: /bɑːn/ *n.* 谷仓，粮仓

② **scrawny**: /ˈskrɔːni/ *adj.* 干瘦的；瘦巴巴的

③ **celebrate**: /ˈselɪbreɪt/ *v.* 庆祝；庆贺

④ **wedding**: /ˈwedɪŋ/ *n.* 婚礼；结婚庆典

⑤ **reasonable**: /ˈriːznəbl/ *adj.* 公平的；合理的

⑥ **intelligent**: /ɪnˈtelɪdʒənt/ *adj.* 有才智的；聪明的

⑦ **threatening**: /ˈθretnɪŋ/ *adj.* 威胁的；恐吓的

69. 叼着肉的狗

有只**狗**叼着一块**肉**渡河。他看到水中自己的倒影，以为那是另一条狗叼着一块更大的肉。于是，他扑到水中，想去抢那块更大的肉。结果，水中的那块肉根本就不存在，而他嘴里的那块肉又被河水给冲走了。

贪婪会让我们失去更多东西。

The Dog with a Piece of Meat in His Mouth

A dog was crossing a river with a piece of meat in his mouth. When he happened to see his own reflection, he thought it was another dog with a larger piece of meat. So he jumped into the river to grab the meat. As a result, the piece of meat in the water did not exist at all, while his own piece of meat was taken away by the river.

Greed will make us lose more.

70. 挂铃铛的狗

有条**狗**常常无故咬人，主人就在他的脖子上挂了一个**铃铛**，好让人们防范着他。可狗却戴着铃铛在市场上跑来跑去，十分得意。一只老狗看到了，便对他说："你有什么好得意的？你挂着铃铛并不是因为你有多勇敢或做了好事得到奖励，而是你做了很多坏事得让大家知道。"

爱吹嘘的人往往会暴露自己藏起来的恶。

想一想

◎ 试想一下，你有没有过像这只挂铃铛的狗一样，做错了事而不自知？

The Dog with a Bell

There was a dog who used to bite people for no good reason. His master tied a bell round his neck so that everyone would know when he was coming. The dog then paraded① about the marketplace, shaking his bell back and forth②. An old dog saw that and said to him, " Why are you acting so proud of yourself ? The bell is not a reward③ for bravery or good behaviour④, but a badge of disgrace."

People who love to brag often reveal their hidden notoriety⑤.

① **parade**: /pəˈreɪd/ *v.* 游行；招摇过市

② **forth**: /fɔːθ/ *adv.* 向前；向某处

③ **reward**: /rɪˈwɔːd/ *n.* 奖励；奖赏

④ **behaviour**: /bɪˈheɪvjə/ *n.* 行为；举止

⑤ **notoriety**: /ˌnəʊtəˈraɪəti/ *n.* 恶名；臭名昭著

71. 猎狗与狐狸

有只**猎狗**看见了狮子，便追了上去。可当狮子回头对他吼叫时，他吓得掉头就跑。

狐狸见状说道：“啊，胆小的猎狗，你连狮子的吼叫都害怕，你还追狮子干吗？”

那些总在表现自己十分强大的人，可能在真正的强者面前不堪一击。

The Hound and the Fox

A hound spied a lion and then chased him with all his might. But when the lion turned around and roared[①] at him, the hound immediately abandoned[②] his pursuit, turned around, and ran away.

A fox happened to see the hound and said, " Why would you chase after a lion when you cannot even stand his roar?"

Those who are always showing that they are very strong may be vulnerable[③] to the real strong.

---

① **roar**: /rɔː/ *v./ n.*吼叫；咆哮

② **abandon**: /əˈbændən/ *v.* 离弃；放弃；遗弃；抛弃

③ **vulnerable**: /ˈvʌlnrəbl/ *adj.* 脆弱的，易受伤害的；易受影响的

72. 蚊子与狮子

一只**蚊子**来到一只**狮子**面前说道："我可一点儿都不怕你。你除了用你的大力气舞几下爪子，摆弄几下牙齿，没什么了不起。你敢不敢跟我比试比试？"说完，蚊子吹着喇叭，猛冲过去，专咬狮子那没长毛的鼻头。狮子被惹得一通乱抓，最后抓花了脸，只好求饶。蚊子战胜了狮子，得意地吹起喇叭在空中飞着。一不小心，他粘在了蛛网上。蚊子哀叹道："我已经战胜了那么强壮的狮子，却要被小小的蜘蛛吃掉。"

人能战胜比自己强大的人，却也可能败给不起眼的对手。

想一想

◎ 在这个故事里，蚊子有什么优点，又有什么缺点？

The Mosquito[①] and the Lion

A mosquito came to the lion and said, " I do not fear you at all. You can only scratch[②] with your claws[③] and bite with your teeth. You are not remarkable. If you agree, let's go and fight it out." The mosquito sounded his trumpet and charged, biting the lion's nose which was not covered with hair. The lion could only wear himself out[④] with his claws until he finally admitted defeat. Succeeded in defeating the lion, the mosquito sounded his trumpet again. He then flew away, only to get entangled in the web of a spider[⑤]. The mosquito lamented, " I have defeated such a powerful lion, but I will be eaten by an insignificant[⑥] spider."

People can defeat those who are stronger than themselves, and they can also lose to those who are insignificant.

---

① **mosquito**: /məˈskiːtəʊ/ *n.* 蚊子

② **scratch**: /skrætʃ/ *v.* 抓；挠；搔

③ **claw**: /klɔː/ *n.* （兽类或鸟类的）爪，脚爪

④ **wear sb. out**: 使某人筋疲力尽

⑤ **spider**: /ˈspaɪdə/ *n.* 蜘蛛

⑥ **insignificant**: /ˌɪnsɪgˈnɪfɪknt/ *adj.* 不重要的；无足轻重的

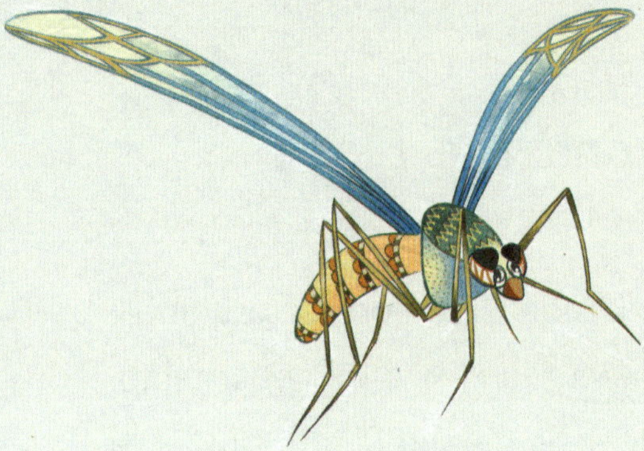

73. 蚊子与公牛

蚊子停在**公牛**的角上休息了好久。当他想离开的时候，他问公牛是不是希望自己能早点走开。

公牛回答："你来的时候我并不知道，所以你什么时候走，我也没必要知道。"

那些既不会带来好处又不会带来坏处的人，他们存不存在，并不会引起人们的注意。

The Mosquito and the Bull

A mosquito landed on the horn of a bull and rested there for a long time. When he decided to leave, he asked the bull if he wished he could go away sooner.

The bull replied, " I did not notice when you came, so I don't care when you are leaving."

The existence[1] of those who bring neither benefits[2] nor disadvantages[3] will not attract[4] people's attention.

① **existence**: /ɪɡˈzɪstns/ *n.* 存在；实有

② **benefit**: /ˈbenɪfɪt/ *n.* 利益，好处；优势

③ **disadvantage**: /ˌdɪsədˈvɑːntɪdʒ/ *n.* 劣势，不利因素

④ **attract**: /əˈtrækt/ *v.* 吸引；使喜爱

74. 兔子与青蛙

有一回，**兔子**们聚在一起，为自己的胆小和无能难过，又为常常受到其他动物的追杀而悲伤。他们都觉得，与其担惊受怕地活着，不如早早地死去。

于是他们一起奔向池塘，想要投水自尽。这时，一群围坐在池塘边的**青蛙**听见了急促的奔跑声，转眼全都跳入水中。一只兔子看到这一切后，仿佛明白了什么，对同伴们说道："朋友们，我们没必要死了。你们快看，这世上还有比我们更胆小的动物呢！"

不幸的人往往会用别人的不幸安慰自己。

想一想

◎ 在这个故事里，兔子们最不幸的一点是什么？

The Rabbits and the Frogs

Once, the rabbits got together, feeling sad for their timidity[1] and incompetence[2], and for always being chased by other animals. They all decided that it was better to die early than to live in fear.

So they headed for the pond, intending to take their own lives. At this moment, the frogs who sat on the bank of the pond heard the noise that the rabbits made, and scampered[3] into the water. One of the rabbits saw what happened. He seemed to understand something and called out to his companions, "All my friends, we don't have to die. Look, there are creatures who are even more cowardly[4] than us!"

Unhappy people often comfort[5] themselves with the misfortunes of others.

---

① **timidity**: /tɪˈmɪdəti/ *n.* 胆小

② **incompetence**: /ɪnˈkɒmpɪtns/ *n.* 无能力；不胜任，不称职

③ **scamper**: /ˈskæmpə/ *v.* 欢快地奔走；蹦蹦跳跳

④ **cowardly**: /ˈkaʊədli/ *adj.* 胆小的；懦弱的

⑤ **comfort**: /ˈkʌmfət/ *v.* 安慰；抚慰；宽慰

75. 老狮子与狐狸

有只**狮子**又老又虚弱，抓不到食物的他想出了一个办法。他钻进一个山洞里，装成生病的样子。等一些动物过来看望老狮子时，他便一口将他们吃掉。

有一天，来了一只**狐狸**，却只是远远地站在洞外询问老狮子的身体有没有好转。老狮子回答："我的身体还是那么糟糕。你为什么不进来看看我呢？"狐狸回答："我本来也想进去探望你。可我发现了很多走进山洞的脚印，却找不到一个离开山洞的脚印。"

聪明的人可以发现线索，从而成功躲避危险。

The Old Lion and the Fox

A lion had grown old and weak, and could not hunt any more. So he came up with an idea. He went into a cave and pretended[①] to be sick. When the animals come and pay their respects he could eat them all up.

One day, a fox came to see the lion, but he just greeted[②] him from outside of the cave, asking the lion how he did. The old lion said, "My body is still that bad. Why don't you come in?" The fox replied, "I really wanted to visit you in the cave, if I hadn't noticed that all the footprints[③] point towards the cave and none the other way."

Smart people can find clues[④] to avoid danger.

---

① **pretend**: /prɪˈtend/ *v.* 假装；佯装

② **greet**: /griːt/ *v.* 和（某人）打招呼（或问好）；迎接

③ **footprint**: /ˈfʊtprɪnt/ *n.* 脚印；足迹

④ **clue**: /kluː/ *n.* 线索，迹象

76. 恋爱的狮子与农夫

狮子爱上了**农夫**的女儿。可农夫并不想将女儿嫁给一只野兽，又因为害怕狮子而不敢拒绝。农夫便想出了一个办法。当狮子再来提亲时，农夫就对狮子说："你非常适合做我女儿的新郎。可如果你不肯拔掉你的牙齿和爪子，我女儿是不会嫁给你的。因为她十分害怕这些东西。"恋爱中的狮子听信了农夫的话，拔掉了牙齿和爪子。但从那之后，农夫再也不害怕狮子了，他甚至走到狮子跟前，用棍子把狮子赶走了。

轻信不值得信任的人会让我们失去最重要的东西，还会被轻易打败。

想一想

◎ 如果你是这只狮子，你会用什么方式打动农夫，顺利娶到农夫的女儿呢？

The Lion in Love and the Farmer

A lion fell in love with the farmer's daughter. But the farmer did not want to marry his daughter to a beast①. However, he was too afraid to refuse the lion. Then the farmer came up with an idea. When the lion came again, he said to the lion, " You are very suitable② to be the husband of my daughter. But she will not marry you unless you have your teeth and claws removed, because she is afraid of them very much. The lion was so in love with the woman that he agreed to pull out his teeth and claws. From then on, the farmer no longer feared the lion, and he even approached the lion and drove him away with his club③.

Credulity④ in those who are not worth trust will cause us to lose the most important things and be easily defeated.

① **beast**: /biːst/ *n.* （尤指大型或野生的）动物；野兽

② **suitable**: /ˈsuːtəbl/ *adj.* 合适的；适宜的

③ **club**: /klʌb/ *n.* （用作武器的）棍，棒

④ **credulity**: /krəˈdjuːləti/ *n.* 轻信

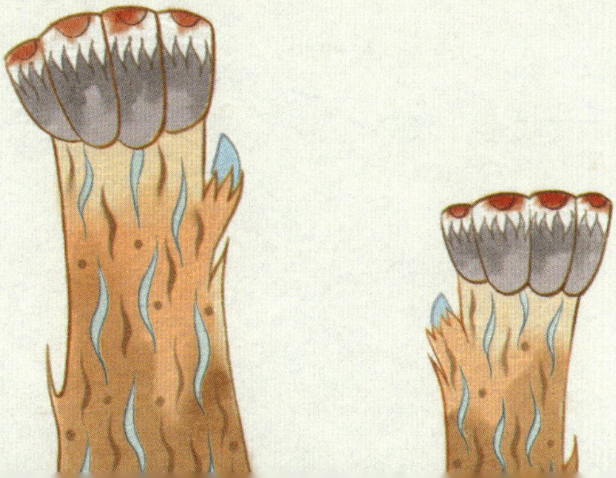

77. 狮子与海豚

狮子在海边散步，看见一只**海豚**从海中探出头来，他便对海豚说："我们一个是陆地上的王，一个是海洋里的王，我们应当成为朋友，互相帮助。"海豚高兴地答应了。

当狮子和野牛打仗时，他请海豚来帮忙。海豚虽然点头了，可始终没有上岸。狮子便指责海豚背叛朋友。

海豚回答："这可不能责怪我，你要怪大自然，它让我成为不能上岸的海洋生物。"

遇到困难时，不要一味指责朋友不帮忙，也要站在朋友的立场想一想。

The Lion and the Dolphin[①]

A lion was wandering[②] on the seashore when he saw a dolphin stick his head out of the water. The lion said to the dolphin, " I rule all the animals on the land, while you are the king of the sea creatures, so we should be friends and assist each other." The dolphin happily agreed.

Not long afterwards, the lion had a war with the wild bull. He asked the dolphin for help. Although agreed to help, the dolphin did not come out of the sea. The lion accused him of betrayal.

The dolphin replied, " You can't blame me for this. You should blame the nature who made me a sea creature that cannot come out onto the land."

Don´t accuse a friend of offering no help, but think in his shoes.

---

① **dolphin**: /ˈdɒlfɪn/ *n.* 海豚

② **wander**: /ˈwɒndə/ *v.* 漫游；游荡；闲逛

78. 狮子与野猪

一个炎热的夏天，**狮子**和**野猪**来到一处泉水边。他们为谁先去喝水争得你死我活。突然，他们发现身后站着几只秃鹰，随时准备吃掉战败的一方。

狮子和野猪马上停止了争斗。他们觉得比起变成秃鹰的食物，还是成为彼此的朋友更加划算。

无端的争斗会招来不幸。

想一想

◎ 狮子与野猪的故事还告诉了我们什么道理呢？

The Lion and the Boar[①]

On a hot summer day, a lion and a wild boar came to a spring. They began to argue about which one of them should take the first drink, and their argument escalated[②] into a fight to the death. When they paused[③] to catch their breath, they saw some vultures[④] waiting behind them , ready to eat up the one who was killed.

They stopped the fight at once, because they thought it was better for them to be friends than to be eaten by vultures.

Unprovoked[⑤] fighting will bring misfortune.

---

① **boar**: /bɔː/ *n.* 野猪；未阉的公猪

② **escalate**: /ˈeskəleɪt/ *v.* （使）扩大；（使）加剧

③ **pause**: /pɔːz/ *v.* 暂停；停顿

④ **vulture**: /ˈvʌltʃə/ *n.* 兀鹫；秃鹫

⑤ **unprovoked**: /ˌʌnprəˈvəʊkt/ *adj.* 无端的，无缘无故的

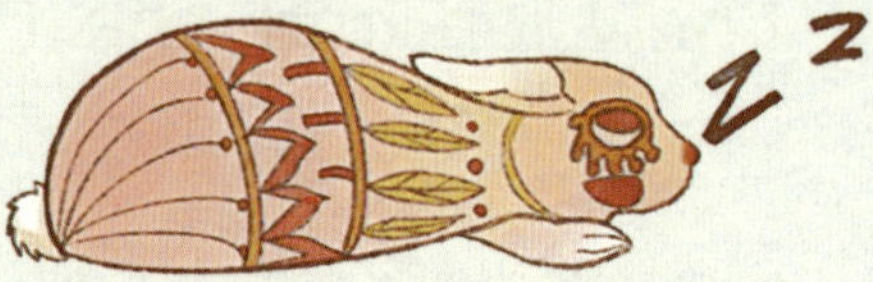

79. 狮子与兔子

有只**狮子**遇见一只睡着的**兔子**，正当狮子准备张开大嘴时，又看到了不远处的一只小鹿。狮子便丢下兔子去追小鹿。

可小鹿听到了狮子的脚步声，逃跑了。狮子追了很久，始终没抓到小鹿，于是他又原路返回，但之前那只睡着的兔子也不见了。

狮子懊悔地说道：“我真活该，丢了到手的食物，去追会逃跑的猎物。”

那些不知足的人终将一无所有。

The Lion and the Hare[①]

A lion found a hare sleeping in the wood. Just as he was about to devour him, the lion happened to catch sight of a passing deer. Left the hare, he ran off chasing after the deer.

Hearing the noise, the deer leaped up and bounded away. The lion chased for a long time but failed to catch the deer. So he came back to where he had left the hare and discovered that the hare had also slipped away.

On finding that, the lion exclaimed, " It serves me right. I went after some prey on the run, but lost the food that was already within my grasp[②]."

Those who are insatiable[③] will eventually have nothing.

① **hare**: /heə/ *n.* 野兔

② **grasp**: /grɑːsp/ *n.* 紧抓；紧握

③ **insatiable**: /inˈseiʃəbl/ adj.不知足的；贪得无厌的

80. 狮子与报恩的老鼠

狮子睡着时，一只**老鼠**不小心从狮子身上经过。狮子一把抓住这只不幸的老鼠，想要吃掉他。老鼠立马求饶说，如果狮子肯放了自己，将来他会报答的。狮子大笑一声，放掉了老鼠。

不久后，老鼠果然救了狮子一命。那时，狮子被猎人抓住，绑在一棵大树上。老鼠听到了狮子的哀号，咬断绳子让狮子逃走了。老鼠对狮子说道："以前你还笑话我，现在知道了吧，就算是老鼠也能报恩的。"

有时强大的人也会需要弱者的帮助。

The Lion and the Mouse Who Repaid[1]

Once a mouse accidentally ran over the lion who was sleeping. The lion woke up and immediately grabbed the wretched[2] little mouse, and wanted to devour him. The mouse begged for mercy[3], saying that he would repay his kindness in the future. The lion laughed and let him go.

A few days later, the mouse really saved the lion's life. The lion was trapped by the hunter and tied to a big tree. The mouse heard the lion's angry roaring and came. He gnawed[4] at the cords[5] and set him free. The mouse said to the lion, " You laughed at me back then, now you know that even a mouse could repay."

Sometimes the strong also need the help of the weak.

---

① **repay**: /rɪˈpeɪ/ *v.* 偿还；报答

② **wretched**: /ˈretʃɪd/ *adj.* 不幸的

③ **mercy**: /ˈmɜːsi/ *n.* 慈悲，怜悯；仁慈，宽容

④ **gnaw**: /nɔː/ *v.* 咬；啃；啮

⑤ **cord**: /kɔːd/ *n.* （一段）绳，索，线

81. 狮子、驴子与狐狸

狮子、驴子和狐狸一起结伴去打猎。他们抓到了很多猎物，狮子命令驴子来分配。驴子将食物平均分成三份，让大家来拿。狮子气得直接把驴子吞进了肚子。狮子又命令狐狸来分配，狐狸只给自己留了一小份，把剩下的所有的食物都献给了狮子。狮子问狐狸谁教他分得这么好。狐狸回答，是驴子的死教会自己这些的。

要懂得从别人的失误中汲取经验。

想一想

◎ 你觉得狐狸做对了什么，又做错了什么？

The Lion, the Donkey and the Fox

The lion, the donkey and the fox went hunting together. Having caught a lot of prey, the lion told the donkey to divide① the spoils②. The donkey then divided them into three equal③ parts for three of them. The lion was so enraged④ that he swallowed the donkey directly into his stomach. The lion then ordered the fox to do the division. The fox only took a small portion⑤ for himself and left all the others to the lion. The lion asked the fox who taught him to do such a good job. The fox replied that it was the death of the donkey that taught him.

Learn from the other's misfortunes.

---

① **divide**: /dɪˈvaɪd/ *v.* 分开；分配

② **spoils**: /spɔɪls/ *n.* 战利品；掠夺物

③ **equal**: /ˈiːkwəl/ *adj.* （大小、数量）相同的，相等的

④ **enrage**: /ɪnˈreɪdʒ/ *v.* 使非常愤怒；激怒

⑤ **portion**: /ˈpɔːʃn/ *n.* 部分；一份

82. 狮子、老鼠与狐狸

一只狮子在窝里睡觉，有只**老鼠**跑到**狮子**身上，把他吵醒了。狮子马上站起来，到处找那只老鼠。**狐狸**看见了，嘲笑狮子竟然害怕老鼠。狮子回道："我不是怕那只老鼠，我只是无法忍受他对我竟然如此无礼。"

轻微的放肆也会被认为是巨大的冒犯。

The Lion, the Mouse and the Fox

A lion was asleep in his den①. A mouse ran over his mane② and woke him. The lion rose up, and searched every corner of his den for the mouse. A fox saw that and made fun of him, saying that he was frightened of a little mouse. The lion said to the fox, " I was not afraid of the mouse. I just can't stand his rude behaviour."

Slight liberties③ can be great offences④.

① **den**: /den/ *n.* （动物的）巢穴，窝

② **mane**: /meɪn/ *n.* （狮子或马等动物颈上的）鬃毛

③ **liberty**: /ˈlɪbəti/ *n.* 自由；放肆，无礼

④ **offence**: /əˈfens/ *n.* 罪行；冒犯；得罪

83. 狼与小羊

狼看见一只小羊在河边喝水，便想找个理由吃掉他。于是狼明明站在上游，却责备小羊把河水弄浑了，让自己喝不了水。小羊说道，自己并没有站在河里喝水，而且又是处在河的下游，是不会把上游的水弄脏的。狼只好说："但你去年骂过我的父亲。"小羊继续说："那时我都还没出生呢。"最后狼对小羊说道："即使你辩解得再好，我也不会放过你的。"

对于那些一心想做坏事的人，无论怎么讲道理都是没有用的。

The Wolf and the Lamb[①]

A wolf once saw a lamb drinking water by the river and wanted to find an excuse to eat him. Standing upstream[②], the wolf blamed the lamb for making the river muddy[③] that he was unable to drink. The lamb said he was not standing in the river, and he was in the lower part of the river which couldn't get the water dirty up there. The wolf then said, " You insulted[④] my father last year." The lamb continued, " I was not born yet." Finally, the wolf said to the lamb, " You are not going to make this wolf go without his dinner, even though you are able to refute[⑤] every one of his charges[⑥]."

To those who resolve to do bad things, it is useless to reason with them[⑦].

---

① **lamb**: /læm/ *n.* 羊羔；小羊

② **upstream**: /ˌʌpˈstriːm/ *adv.* 向（或在）上游；逆流

③ **muddy**: /ˈmʌdi/ *adj.* 泥泞的；浑浊的

④ **insult**: /ɪnˈsʌlt/ *v.* 辱骂，侮辱

⑤ **refute**: /rɪˈfjuːt/ *v.* 驳斥；反驳

⑥ **charge**: /tʃɑːdʒ/ *n.* 指控，指责

⑦ **reason with sb.**: 与某人讲道理；说服某人；规劝某人

84. 狼与鹤

狼的喉咙里卡了一根骨头，到处求助。狼遇到了鹤，于是说要给他报酬，请他帮忙取出骨头。鹤便把自己的头伸到狼的嘴里，拔出了骨头，之后就向狼索要那约定的报酬。

狼答道："喂，伙计，你能从狼的嘴里平安无事地把头缩回去，还要来讨报酬？"

狡诈之人的话不可信。

想一想

◎ 如果你是那只鹤，接下来你会怎么做？

The Wolf and the Crane[1]

A wolf got a bone stuck in his throat[2]. He looked everywhere for help. Then the wolf met a crane. He asked the crane to help him remove the bone and promised him a reward. The crane, convinced[3] by the wolf, put his head into the mouth of the wolf and pulled out the bone, and then demanded[4] the promised reward.

The wolf said, " Hey, buddy, you extracted[5] your head in safety from the mouth of a wolf and you still asked for a reward?"

Do not believe the words told by the cunning[6] ones.

---

① **crane**: /kreɪn/ *n.* 鹤；起重机，吊车

② **throat**: /θrəʊt/ *n.* 咽喉；喉咙

③ **convince**: /kənˈvɪns/ *v.* 使确信；使相信

④ **demand**: /dɪˈmɑːnd/ *v.* 强烈要求；需要

⑤ **extract**: /ɪkˈstrækt/ *v.* 取出；拔出；提取

⑥ **cunning**: /ˈkʌnɪŋ/ *adj.* 狡猾的，狡诈的

85. 狼与狮子

有一回，**狼**从羊舍中偷了一只羊，准备叼回自己的窝。半道上，**狮子**钻了出来，把羊抢走了。狼远远地站着，说道：“你抢我的东西是不对的。”狮子却笑着说道：“那么你的羊是朋友送的吗？”

换种方式做坏事没有区别。

The Wolf and the Lion

Once a wolf stole a sheep from the flock and was carrying it on the way home when he ran into a lion. The lion took the sheep away from him and walked off with it. The wolf stood at a distance ① and said, " It's not right for you to snatch my things." The lion laughed and called out in reply, " Then your sheep was given by a friend?"

There is no difference of doing evil in another way.

① **distance**: /ˈdɪstəns/ *n.* 距离；间距

86. 狼与驴子

有只**狼**成了狼群的首领之后制定了一条法律：狼群猎得的食物必须平均分给每一只狼，这样大家就不会因为缺少食物而自相残杀了。

这时，一头**驴子**走了过来，他摆着鬃毛说道：“阁下立的法律固然是好，可你为什么又把昨晚抓到的猎物藏进自己的窝里呢？快拿出来和大家分享吧。”被驴子揭穿之后，那只狼感到很惭愧，便把法律废除了。

说一套做一套，终究会被揭穿。

想一想

◎ 如果狼制定的法律被你识破了，你会选择沉默着遵守，还是告诉其他同伴这个秘密？

The Wolf and the Donkey

There was a wolf who ruled over the others and decreed① that whatever they might catch while hunting would be kept in common② and divided equally by the whole pack.

At this time, a donkey came over, shaking his mane and said," The law you made is good, but why did you hide the prey you caught last night in your den? Take it out and share it with others." Having been exposed by the donkey, the wolf felt ashamed and abolished③ the law he had made.

People who talk in one way but act in another will be exposed at last.

---

① **decree**: /dɪˈkriː/ *v.* 裁定；判决；颁布

② **common**: /ˈkɒmən/ *adj.* 常见的；共有的

③ **abolish**: /əˈbɒlɪʃ/ *v.* 废除，废止

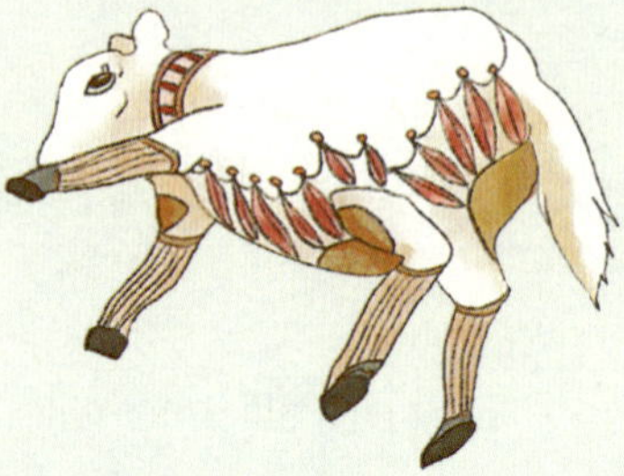

87. 吃饱的狼与羊

有只**吃饱的狼**看见了一只倒在地上的**羊**。狼觉得是因为羊看到自己太害怕而起不来身，便上前鼓励他。狼告诉羊，只要说出三句真话，就可以放他走。

羊先是告诉狼自己一点也不想遇上他。接着羊又说，希望现在遇上的这只狼是个瞎眼的。最后羊说道："祈求所有的恶狼都没有好下场。因为我们从不伤害他们，他们却总来伤害我们。"

狼认为羊说的都是真话，便真的放了他。

有时真诚甚至能打动敌人。

The Wolf with a Full Stomach and the Sheep

A wolf with a full stomach saw a sheep lying on the ground. The wolf thought that the sheep couldn't get up because he was too scared, so he stepped forward to encourage[①] him. The wolf told the sheep that he would let him go as long as he told three truths.

The sheep first told the wolf that he didn't want to meet him at all. Then the sheep continued that he hoped the wolf he met was a blind one. At last the sheep said, " I pray that all the evil wolves will not end well. Because we never hurt them, but they always hurt us."

The wolf thought the sheep was telling the truth, so he really let him go.

Sometimes sincerity[②] can even impress[③] an enemy.

---

① **encourage**: /ɪnˈkʌrɪdʒ/ *v.* 鼓励；激励

② **sincerity**: /sɪnˈserəti/ *n.* 诚实，真诚

③ **impress**: /ɪmˈpres/ *v.* 使钦佩；给……留下深刻印象

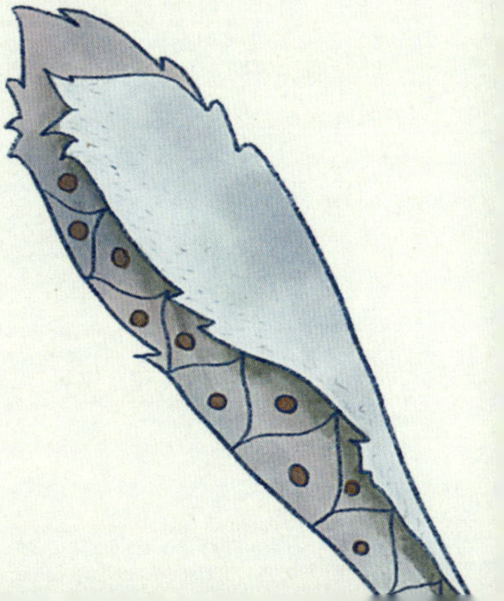

88. 受伤的狼与羊

有只狼被狗咬了，受了很严重的伤倒在地上。这时一只羊路过，狼便求他去河边给自己打点水。狼还对羊说：“只要我喝上一口水，我就有力气去找食物了。”羊却回答：“如果你喝上一口水，你就有力气把我当成食物了吧。”

帮助恶人就是在伤害自己。

想一想

◎ 面对受伤的敌人，我们该不该伸出援手？

The Injured[1] Wolf and the Sheep

A wolf mauled[2] by dogs fell down on the ground. At this time a sheep passed by. The wolf begged him to fetch some water from the river. The wolf also said to the sheep, " If you bring me some water, I will find myself something to eat." The sheep replied, "But if I give you something to drink, you would doubtless make me your dinner, too."

He who helps the wicked is hurting himself.

---

① **injure**: /ˈɪndʒə/ *v.* 伤害；损害

② **maul**: /mɔːl/ *v.*（动物用齿或爪子）袭击；伤害

89. 灯

灌满了油的**灯**发出耀眼的光芒，他夸耀自己比太阳还亮堂。不料一阵风瞬间将他吹灭。

有人再次将灯点亮，并对他说道："灯啊，踏踏实实地照着吧。别说太阳了，就连星星都不需要别人去把它们重新点亮。"

夜郎自大，实在可笑。

The Lamp[1]

A lamp filled with oil glowed[2] brightly. He boasted that he gave more light than the sun. A sudden puff[3] of wind extinguished[4] the lamp.

A man lit the lamp once again and said to him, " Lamp, just keep alight. Never mind the sun. Even the stars don't need to be relit."

It´s ludicrous[5] to boast without knowing that the others are much greater than you.

① **lamp**: /læmp/ *n.* 灯

② **glow**: /gləʊ/ *v.* 发光；发热

③ **puff**: /pʌf/ *n.* （烟、气等的）一缕；一股

④ **extinguish**: /ɪkˈstɪŋgwɪʃ/ *v.* 熄灭，扑灭（火或光）

⑤ **ludicrous**: /ˈluːdɪkrəs/ *adj.* 愚蠢可笑的；荒谬的

90. 蜜蜂与宙斯

蜜蜂舍不得自己的蜜，便祈求**宙斯**能赐给自己力量，把靠近蜂窝的人都刺死。宙斯对这个歹毒的愿望十分生气，但又不想拒绝蜜蜂的请求，于是便给了蜜蜂新的能力：他可以用刺伤人，但是只要他刺了人，他的刺就会断掉，他的性命也因此会丢掉。

伤害别人，自己也不会有什么好下场。

知识岛：宙斯

◎ 宙斯是希腊神话中的天空之神和众神之王。相传，当他心情好的时候，天空就会阳光明媚；当他愤怒的时候，天上就会电闪雷鸣。

The Bee and Zeus

A bee, who did not want his honey to be taken away by people, prayed to Zeus that he would give him strength to strike[①] everyone close to the honeycomb to death. Zeus was much displeased with this vicious[②] desire but did not want to refuse him either. So he gave the bee a new ability[③]: he could attack a person with his sting[④] if they approach for his honey, but his sting would break and he will die from the loss of it.

Hurting others may get ourselves into danger.

---

① **strike**: /straɪk/ *v.* 撞；碰；撞击；碰撞；打；击打

② **vicious**: /ˈvɪʃəs/ *adj.* 狂暴的；充满仇恨的

③ **ability**: /əˈbɪləti/ *n.* 能力；才能

④ **sting**: /stɪŋ/ *n.* 刺

91. 老鼠与黄鼠狼

老鼠和**黄鼠狼**打仗，总是失败。老鼠们便聚在一起商量，觉得失败的原因是没有指挥战事的将领。于是他们选出了几只老鼠作为将领。被选作将领的老鼠为了显示自己的与众不同，便用羽毛做了些装饰戴在自己的头上。

与黄鼠狼的战斗又开始了，老鼠们还是打不过，就都躲回了洞里。可那些老鼠将领因为头上戴了装饰没能钻回洞里，一只只被黄鼠狼捉住吃掉了。

过度虚荣只会害了自己。

The Mice and the Weasels[①]

The mice and the weasels were at war with each other, and the mice lose every battle[②]. They gathered together to discuss and realized that the reason for their failures[③] was that they had no generals[④] to command[⑤] them. So several mice were elected generals. The newly-elected generals wanted to be more conspicuous[⑥] from the rank and file[⑦], so they decorated their heads with some feathers.

Then another battle began and the mice were defeated again. Most of the mice easily slipped into the mouse holes. The commanders, however, were unable to get inside because of their head dresses, and were all captured and eaten by the weasels.

Superfluous[⑧] vanity will bring us misfortune.

---

① **weasel**: /ˈwiːzl/ *n.* 鼬；黄鼠狼

② **battle**: /bætl/ *n* 战斗；战役；战争

③ **failure**: /ˈfeɪljə/ *n.* 失败；失败的人（或事）

④ **general**: /ˈdʒenrl/ *n.* 将军

⑤ **command**: /kəˈmɑːnd/ *v.* 命令；指挥；统帅

⑥ **conspicuous**: /kənˈspɪkjuəs/ *adj.* 明显的；惹人注意的

⑦ **rank and file**: 普通成员；普通士兵

⑧ **superfluous**: /suːˈpɜːfluəs/ *adj.* 过多的；多余的

92. 苍蝇

苍蝇掉进了在盛满肉汤的碗里。在快要被肉汤淹死的时候，他对自己说道："我已经吃饱喝足了，还洗了一次澡，就算死了也无憾了。"

人们容易自我麻痹。

知识岛：阿Q精神

◎ 鲁迅写过一个名叫《阿Q正传》的故事。故事中的阿Q和这只苍蝇一样，已经陷入了巨大的麻烦，还不忘自我陶醉与自我安慰，干出了许多啼笑皆非的事。人们便把这样的处事态度称为"阿Q精神"。

The Fly

A fly fell into a bowl full of broth[①]. When he was about to be drowned, he said to himself, " I have eaten and drunk enough, and also taken a bath. Even if I die, I have no regrets."

People tend to numb themselves emotionally to avoid pain.

---

① **broth**: /brɒθ/ *n.*（加入蔬菜的）肉汤

93. 挥霍无度的年轻人与燕子

一个**挥霍无度的年轻人**把所有的家产都挥霍光了，只剩下一件外衣。他见到一只早早就回来的**燕子**，以为春天到了，便把外衣也拿去卖了。可风雪交加的日子来了，那人哆嗦着看见了燕子冻死的尸体，对其说道："喂，朋友，你不仅害了自己，还害了我。"

一燕不成夏。

The Spendthrift[1] and the Swallow[2]

There was a prodigal[3] young man who had run through all his patrimony[4] except one coat. Seeing a swallow coming back earlier, he thought the spring was just around the corner. So he took the coat and sold it. Then a snowstorm[5] came, and he shivered[6] with cold. He saw the dead body of the swallow and said, " Hey, friend, you have not only killed yourself, but destroyed me as well."

One swallow doesn′t make a summer.

---

① **spendthrift**: /ˈspendθrɪft/ *n.* 挥霍者，花钱无度的人

② **swallow**: /ˈswɒləʊ/ *n.* 燕子

③ **prodigal**: /ˈprɒdɪgl/ *adj.* 浪费的，奢侈的

④ **patrimony**: /ˈpætrɪməni/ *n.* 遗产

⑤ **snowstorm**: /ˈsnəʊstɔːm/ *n.* 暴风雪

⑥ **shiver**: /ˈʃɪvə/ *v.* （因寒冷、疾病或恐惧而）颤抖，发抖

94. 蝙蝠与黄鼠狼

蝙蝠掉在地上，被**黄鼠狼**抓住了，他请求黄鼠狼饶过自己。黄鼠狼说，他不能放过蝙蝠，因为一切鸟都是他的天敌。蝙蝠说自己不是鸟，而是老鼠。黄鼠狼便把他放了。后来，蝙蝠又被另一只黄鼠狼抓住了，他再次请求黄鼠狼放过自己。黄鼠狼说他痛恨所有的老鼠。蝙蝠说自己并不是老鼠，而是鸟，于是他又被黄鼠狼放了。

就这样，蝙蝠改了两次名字，救了自己的性命。

遇到危险时要随机应变。

The Bat and the Weasel

A bat fell upon the ground and was seized by a weasel. The bat begged for mercy but the weasel refused to let him go, claiming that all birds were his enemies. The bat argued that he was not a bird, but a mouse, so the weasel let him go. Later on, the bat was seized again by another weasel. The bat also begged the weasel to release him, but the weasel refused, saying he hated all mice. The bat denied[①] that he was a mouse, but a bird, so once again he was set free.

As a result, the bat was able to save himself twice by changing his name.

Play it by ear[②] when you face with a danger.

---

① **deny**: /dɪˈnaɪ/ *v.* 否认；否定

② **play it by ear**: 见机行事，随机应变

95. 两个旅人与熊

两个旅人走在路上，一只**熊**突然冲到他们面前。其中一个人立马爬上树，躲了起来。另一个人没有别的办法，只好倒在地上装死。那熊走近地上的人，用鼻子嗅了嗅。地上的人憋住了呼吸，因为他听说熊不吃死人。熊就真的抛下那人走了。树上的人马上跳下来问，熊是不是在他耳边说了些什么。地上的人答道："熊说，以后千万不要同那些在危难时抛下你的人一同上路。"

灾难能证明谁是真正的朋友。

想一想

◎ 真正的朋友是什么样子的？

The Two Travellers and the Bear

Two men were travelling in company through a forest when a bear suddenly rushed① out in front of them. One of them climbed quickly up a tree and concealed himself in the branches. The other one had no other choice but fell to the ground, pretending to be dead. The wild beast ran up to him and sniffed②. The man held his breath because he had heard that bears do not touch dead body. The bear really abandoned the man and went away. The man in the tree immediately jumped down and asked if the bear had whispered something in his ear. The man on the ground replied, " The bear said, in the future, never travel with those who would desert③ you in times of danger."

Misfortune is the test of true friendship.

① **rush**: /rʌʃ/ *v.* 冲；（使）急速行进

② **sniff**: /snɪf/ *v.* 嗅，闻

③ **desert**: /dɪˈzɜːt/ *v.* 抛弃；丢弃

96. 驴子与骡子

驴子和**骡子**一起运货。驴子看到骡子背的东西，生气地说这一点都不公平，因为骡子吃了双倍的食物，却和自己背一样重的东西。但他们走了一段路后，商人看见那驴子有点背不动了，便把他背上的重物分了一点给骡子。驴子还是越走越累，身上的重物就被一点点地搬到骡子身上。骡子背上了全部的货物后转头问驴子："喂，朋友，现在你还觉得我吃双倍的食物不公平吗？"

不能仅靠第一印象去判断一个人。

The Donkey and the Mule[①]

A donkey and a mule were carrying goods together. Seeing that they were carrying the equal loads, the donkey got angry and complained that the mule was awarded a double portion of food but carried a load that was no heavier than his. After a while, the businessman saw that the donkey could not go any further, so he took part of the donkey's load and placed it on the mule. However, the donkey grew more tired, the man again transferred[②] some of the donkey's load to the mule. Finally the mule carried the entire load. Then he said to the donkey, " Hey, friend. Do you still think it is unfair for me to have double portion of food?"

Do not judge a person only by the first impression[③].

① **mule**: /mjuːl/ *n.* 骡子

② **transfer**: /trænsˈfɜː/ *v.* 搬；转移

③ **impression**: /ɪmˈpreʃn/ *n.* 印象；感想

97. 父亲与他的两个女儿

一个**父亲**有**两个女儿**，其中一个嫁给了园丁，另一个嫁给了陶工。

过了段时间，他去看望嫁给园丁的女儿，问她生活得如何，有没有需要帮忙的地方。女儿说一切都还不错，只是希望父亲能向上天祷告下场雨，好浇灌园里的植物。

他又去看望嫁给陶工的女儿，问她生活得如何，有没有不顺心的地方。女儿说希望父亲能向上天祷告继续晴天，好晾干更多陶器。

他便对女儿说道："你要晴天，可你的姐妹又要雨天，那么我该为哪一边祷告呢？"

人生很难两全其美，有得必有失。

The Father and His Two Daughters

There was a man who had two daughters, one of whom he married to a gardener[1] and the other to a potter[2].

Some time later, he paid a visit to the daughter married to the gardener, asking how she was and whether she needed any help. The daughter said she was all right, just hoping that her father could pray to gods for some rainfall, so that the plants could be well watered.

The father left and went to see the daughter who was living with the potter. He asked the daughter how she was and what she might need, and the daughter hoped that he could pray for more sunny days so that the pots[3] would dry out more quickly.

Then the father said to his daughter, " You are hoping for sunny days while your sister wants some rain. With which of the two shall I join my wishes?"

You can't make an omelet without breaking eggs.

---

① **gardener**: /ˈɡɑːdnə/ *n.* 花匠；园丁

② **potter**: /ˈpɒtə/ *n.* 陶匠，陶工

③ **pot**: /pɒt/ *n.* 陶碟，陶碗；陶制器皿

98. 两只口袋

相传，人被创造出来之后，又被造物主挂上了**两只口袋**。一只口袋挂在人的胸前，里面装了别人的过错。另一只口袋挂在人的身后，里面装了自己的缺陷。于是，人们总能轻易看见别人的过错，却很难发现自己的缺陷。

人容易紧盯着别人的缺点而忽略自己的过错。

The Two Sacks[1]

According to an ancient legend, human were put two sacks on them after they were created. One sack, which was filled with the faults[2] of others, was hung on the chests of them. While the other one, heavy with their own faults, was hung behind them. This is why we are blind to our own faults but quick to criticise[3] others for their mistakes.

It's easier to focus on others' shortcomings[4] and overlook our own faults.

---

① **sack**: /sæk/ *n.* 大袋子；麻袋

② **fault** /fɔːlt/ *n.* 过错，过失

③ **criticise**: /ˈkrɪtɪsaɪz/ *v.* 批评；批判

④ **shortcoming**: /ˈʃɔːtkʌmɪŋ/ *n.* 缺点；短处

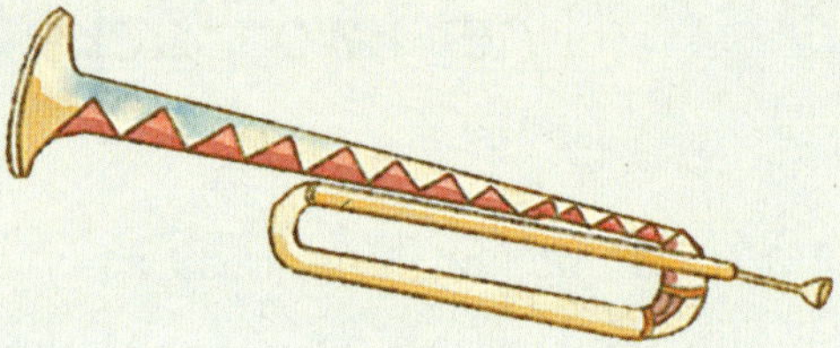

99. 被抓的号兵

有个**号兵**正吹着号召集军队，却被敌人抓住了。号兵大叫："各位，请不要无缘无故地杀我，因为我不曾伤害你们。我除了身上这把铜号，也没有携带任何武器。"但敌人却对他说道："那么你更应当死了，你虽然不能打仗，可是你会喊别人来打仗。"

那些怂恿他人去做恶事的人，更应该受到惩罚。

The Trumpeter[1] Taken Prisoner

A trumpeter was blowing a trumpet to call up his army when he was taken prisoner. The trumpeter shouted, " Please, good sirs, don't kill me for no reason, because I have never killed anyone. I don't have any weapon[2] except this brass[3] trumpet." But the enemy said to him, " That is the reason for which you should be put to death. Although you do not fight, you call on others to fight."

There is more reason to punish[4] those who lead others to evil deeds.

① **trumpeter**: /ˈtrʌmpɪtə/ *n.* 号手；号兵

② **weapon**: /ˈwepən/ *n.* 武器；兵器

③ **brass**: /brɑːs/ *n.* 黄铜；*adj.* 铜管的

④ **punish**: /ˈpʌnɪʃ/ *v.* 处罚；惩罚

100. 狐狸与葡萄

一只饥饿的**狐狸**看到**葡萄**架上挂着大大的葡萄，他非常想吃，于是用尽全力跳起来，却发现自己够不着。于是他转过身，告诉自己那些葡萄都还没熟呢。

人总会对自己得不到的东西摆出一副鄙视的样子。

The Fox and the Grapes

A hungry fox saw some fine bunches of grapes hanging high on the vine[①]. He wanted to eat them very much. He leaped up with all his strength, but could not reach them. At last he turned away and told himself that the grapes were not ripe yet.

It is easy to despise what you cannot get.

① **vine**: /vaɪn/ *n.* 葡萄藤；藤蔓

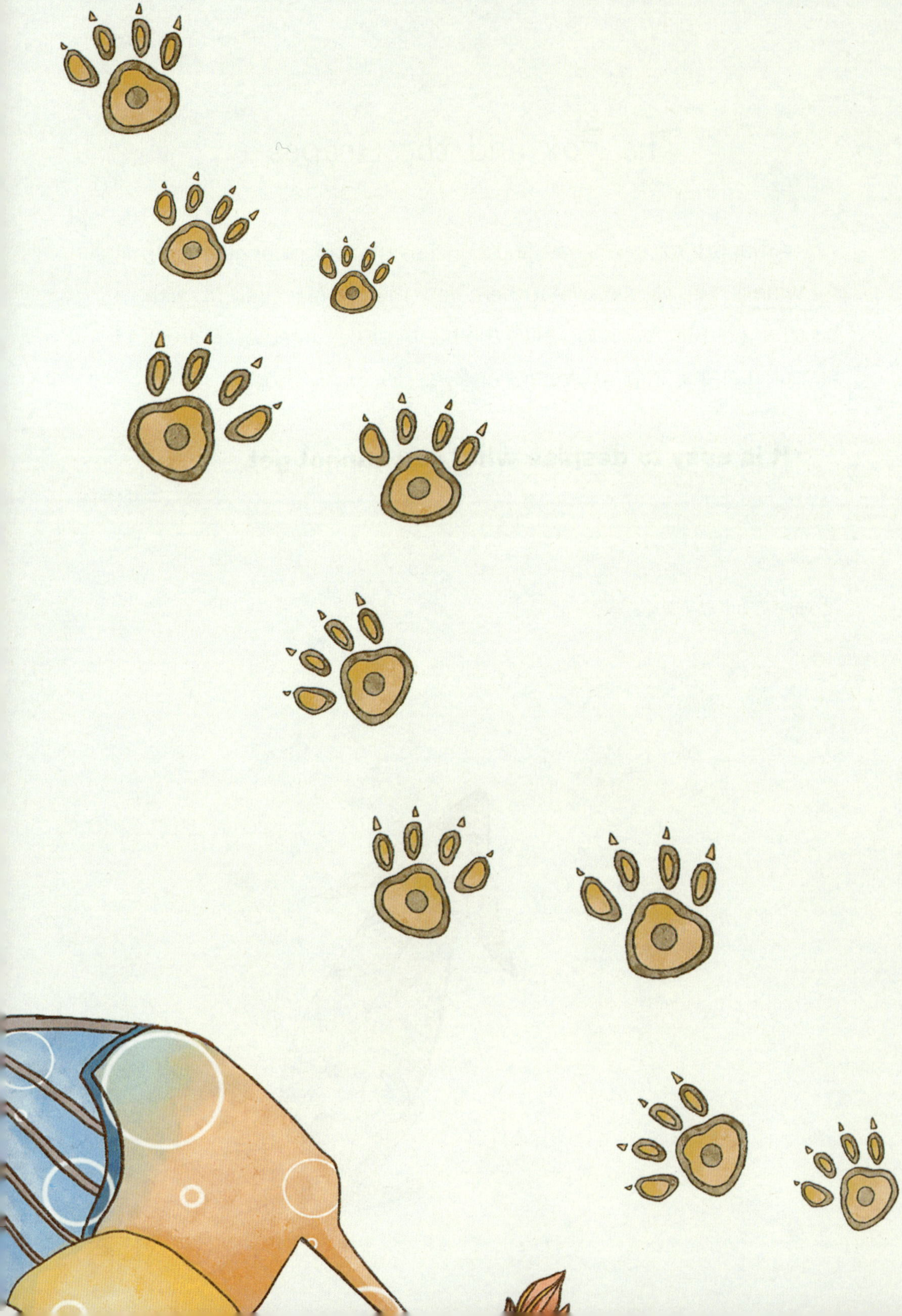